A GUIDE TO CRIMINAL LAW

Revised Edition
Peter Robertson

Editor: Roger Sproston

Emerald Guides
www.straightforwardbooks.co.uk

Emerald Guides

© Straightforward Co Ltd 2023

All rights reserved. No part of this publication may be reproduced in a retrieval system or transmitted by any means, electronic or mechanical, photocopying or otherwise, without the prior permission of the copyright holders.

ISBN

978-1-80236-237-4

Printed by 4edge www.4edge.co.uk

Cover design by Straightforward Graphics

Whilst every effort has been made to ensure that the information contained within this book is correct at the time of going to press, the author and publisher can take no responsibility for the errors or omissions contained within.

CONTENTS

Table of cases	14
Introduction	18
Chapter 1-The Development of Law	**20**
Customs	20
General customs	20
Local customs	21
Common law	21
Equity	22
Judicial precedents	23
The doctrine of precedents	23
Ratio Decidendi	23
Obiter Dicta	24
Original precedent	24
Binding precedent	25
Persuasive precedent	25
The hierarchy of courts and precedent-England and Wales	26
The European Court of Justice	27
The Supreme Court	28
Court of appeal	28
Divisional courts	28
Courts of first instance	28
The High Court	28
Inferior courts	29
Use of Practice Statement	29
Distinguishing, overruling and reversing previous decisions	29
Advantages and disadvantages of precedent in the law	30

Disadvantages	30
The Hierarchy of Courts in Scotland	31
Civil Courts	31
The Supreme Court of the United Kingdom	31
Court of Session	31
Sheriff Court	32
Criminal Courts	32
High Court of Justiciary	32
District Court	32
Justice of the Peace Courts	32
Tribunals and Special Courts:	33
The legal system in Northern Ireland	35
Courts In Northern Ireland	35
Agencies involved in the justice system	36
Reporting cases England and Wales, Scotland and Northern Ireland	36
Chapter 2-The Purpose of Criminal Law	**38**
Defining a crime	38
Sources of criminal law	39
The classification of offences	40
Summary offences	40
Indictable offences	40
Bail and the Policing and Crime Act 2017	41
Bail-the Criminal procedure (Amendment) Act 2023	41
Triable either-way offences	45
Elements of a crime	45
The burden of proof in criminal law	45
Establishing criminal liability	46
The actus reus of a crime	46

State of affairs cases	47
Conduct of the accused	47
Result or consequence	48
Causation	48
Factual causation	49
Legal causation	49
The acceleration principle	50
An omission	50
The Mens Rea of a crime	51
Different degrees of mens rea	52
Crimes of specific intent	52
Crime of basic intent	52
Intention	52
Direct intention	53
Oblique intention	53
Recklessness	54
Cunningham recklessness	55
Caldwell recklessness	55
Negligence	57
Criminal negligence	57
Transferred malice	57
Strict liability	57
Different types of strict liability offences	58
Regulatory offences	58
More serious criminal offences	59

Chapter 3-Homicide-Unlawful Killing — 62

The distinction between murder and manslaughter	62
Murder	62
The definition of murder	63

Current definition of murder	63
Under the Queen's peace	64
Malice aforethought	64
Chain of causation	64
Voluntary manslaughter	66
Diminished responsibility	66
Provocation	67
Evidence of provocation	67
Loss of self-control	68
Reasonable man (normal person) acting in a similar way	69
The survivor of a suicide pact	70
Infanticide	71
Abortion	71
Involuntary manslaughter	72
Constructive (or unlawful act) manslaughter	73
Unlawful act	74
Act must also be dangerous	76
Manslaughter by gross negligence	77
Killing a child or vulnerable adult	78
Corporate manslaughter	78
Causing death by driving	80
Chapter 4-Non-Fatal Offences Against the Person	**81**
Assault	81
Assaults on Emergency Workers	81
Actus reus of assault	82
The threat of assault	82
Mens rea of assault	83
Battery	84
Not all touching is unlawful.	85

Indirect battery	85
The actus reus and mens rea of battery	85
Consent as a defence	86
Actual Bodily Harm	87
Defining actual bodily harm	88
Malicious wounding or grievous bodily harm	88
Harassment and stalking	89
Protection from Stalking Act 2019	90
Harassment	90
Putting the victim in fear of violence	91
Racially or religiously aggravated harassment	91
Northern Ireland	91
Scotland	91

Chapter 5-Sexual offences — 93

Rape	94
Penetration	94
Consent	95
Belief in consent	97
Assault by penetration	97
Sexual in nature	98
Sexual assault	101
Child victims	101
Sexual activity with a child	102

Chapter 6-Property Offences — 103

Theft and other related offences	103
'Things in action'	106
Robbery	106
Burglary	107

Elements of burglary	108
Entry	108
Trespasser	110
Building	110
Aggravated burglary	110
Actus reus	110
Mens rea	111
Criminal Damage	111
Defences to Criminal damage	113
Aggravated criminal damage	115
Arson	115
Damage to computer programmes	116
Chapter 7-Fraud and Non-Payment	**117**
Fraud-Elements of fraud	117
False representation	117
Actus reus	117
Mens rea	118
Untrue or misleading	118
Express or implied	118
Dishonesty	119
Intention to make gain or cause loss	119
Fraud by abuse of position	119
Making off without payment	120
Chapter 8-Cyber Crime	**121**
Cybercrime	121
Cyber-Dependent Crimes	121
Hacking	122
Disruption of Computer Functionality	123

Legislation relating to cyber dependent crimes	125
Cyber-Enabled Crimes	127
Economic Related Cybercrime	128
Fraud	129
Fraud-relevant legislation	131
Intellectual Property Crime (Piracy, Counterfeiting and Forgery)	132
Relevant Legislation	134
The Online Safety Bill	134

Chapter 9-Animal Welfare — 138

The Law and Animal welfare and control of animals	138
The Animal Welfare Act 2006	138
The Animal Welfare (Sentencing) Act 2021	138
Criminal Damage Act 1971	140
The Dangerous Dogs Act 1991	140
Farm animals	142

Chapter 10-Parties to a Crime — 143

The principal offender	143
Secondary offenders	143
To counsel	144
To procure	145
Knowledge that a crime is to be committed	145

Chapter 11-Defences in Criminal Cases — 147

Age and criminal responsibility	147
Children over 10	147
Between ages of ten and fourteen	148
Children of fourteen and over	148

Insanity	149
Unfitness to plead at trial	149
Insanity at the time of the crime	149
Defence of insanity under M'Naughton rules	150
Non-Insane Automatism	150
Intoxication	151
Involuntary intoxication	151
Mistakes about the law	152
Self-defence	152
The Criminal Justice and Immigration Act 2008	153
Necessity	154
Duress	154
Duress of circumstances	154
Marital coercion	155
Public and private defence	155
Chapter 12-Inchoate Offences	**156**
Attempts to commit a crime	156
The actus reus of attempt	156
More than merely preparatory	156
The mens rea of attempt	157
Conspiracy to commit a crime	157
The actus reus of conspiracy	158
The mens rea of conspiracy	158
Incitement	158
The mens rea of incitement	158
Encouraging or assisting crime	159
Liability under the Serious Crime Act 2007	159
Defences of acting reasonably	160
Defences for victims	160

Chapter 13-Criminal Cases-Police Powers 161
Police organisation 161
Police powers 162
Powers to arrest-serious arrestable offences 163
Powers to stop and search 163
Voluntary searches 164
Other powers to stop and search 164
Roadside checks 165
The power to search premises 165
Powers to enter premises without a search warrant 166
To prevent a breach of the peace 166
Searching with the consent of the occupier of the premises 166
Unlawful entry and search 167
Powers of arrest 167
Arrestable offences 167
PACE Section 24- mended by the Serious Organised Crime and Police Act 2005–Arrests by police and private citizens 167
PACE Section 25, as amended by the SOCAP Act 2005 168
Other rights of arrest 168
Arrest for breach of the peace 169
The right to search an arrested person 169
Powers to detain suspect 169
Rights of detained people 170
The right to silence 171
Searches, fingerprints and samples 171
Complaints against the police 172
The Police, Crime, Sentencing and Courts Act 2022 175
The Public Order Act 2023-09-30 176

Chapter 14-Hearing Criminal Cases	**178**
Pre-trial hearings	178
Categories of criminal offences	179
Bail	180
Bail sureties	185
Bail for CPS advice	186
The Crown Prosecution Service	187
Criminal courts	188
The role of the Magistrates Court	188
Summary Trials	189
Triable either-way cases- Plea before venue	190
Sending cases to the Crown Court	191
Committal proceedings	191
Youth courts	191
Appeals from the Magistrates Court	191
Further appeal to the Supreme Court	192
The Crown Court	192
Preliminary matters in the Crown Court-The indictment	193
Disclosure by prosecution and defence	193
The trial	194
Appeals in criminal cases	195
Appeals to the Supreme Court	196
Sentencing	196
Custodial sentences	197
Community sentences	198
Fines	199
The Legal Aid, Sentencing and Punishment of Offenders Act 2012	199
Discharges	200
Other powers available to the courts	200

The Serious Crime Act 2015	201
Offenders who are mentally ill	202
Anti-social behaviour orders	203
New sentencing guidelines for magistrates courts	204

Index

*****

Table of cases

Adamoko 1995 AC 171	77
AG v Whelan 1934 IR 518	154
Anderton and Burnside 1984	104
Arioboke 1998 Crim LR 314	74
B (a minor) v DPP (2000)	61
Bainbridge 1960 1 QB 129	145
Beckford 1988 AC 130	132
Bibby v Chief Constable of Essex 2000	153
Bounekhla 2006	99
Braham 2013	95
Bree 2007	97
Briggs 2003 EWCA Crim 3662	104
Brown 1985 73	109
Caldwell and Lawrence 1982 AC 341	56
Calhaem 1985 QB 808	144
Camplin 1978 AC 705	69
Chamberlaine v Lindon 1998 1 WLR	115
Chan-Fook 1994 1 WLR 689	83
Church 1966 1 QB 59	76
Collins 1973 QB 100	108
Collins and Wilcock 1984 1 WLR	84
Coney 1883 8 QBD 534	86
Costanza 1997	83
Cotswold Geotechnical Holdings Ltd 2012	79
Cunningham 1957 2 QB 396	55
Cunliffe v Goodman 1950 2 KB 237	53
Donnelly v Jackman 1970	84
DPP v Dunn (2000)	91
DPP v Jones	125
DPP v McKeown	125
DPP v Smith (1911)	54

Duffy 1949 1 ALL ER 932	68
Dytham 1939 QB 722	41
Egerton v Harding 1974	21
Gammon (Hong Kong Ltd) v Attorney General	59
G 2009	119
Ghosh 1982	119
Goodfellow 1986 83 Cr App R 23	75
Grewal 2010	95
Hale 1978 68 Cr App R 415	107
Hardie 1985 1 WLR 64	151
Heard 2008	95
Hill v Baxter 1958 1 QB 277	150
Hughes 2013	80
Hunter and Others c Canary Wharf Ltd and LDDC 1995	24
Invicta Plastics Ltd v Clare 1976 RTR 251	158
Instan 1893 1 QB 450	41
Jheeta 2007	97
JM and SM 2012	76
Jaggard v Dickinson 1981 QB 527	114
Johnson 1989	68
Johnson v Youden and Others 1950 1 RB 544	145
Jones 1990 1 WLR 1057	156
Kelly 2003	91
Lamb 1943	74
Larkin 1943 KB 174	73-74
Latimer 1886	57
London Borough of Harrow v Shah and Shah 2000	58
Lou v DPP 2000	90
M and Another 2009	61
Marchant and Muntz 2004	49
Martin 1881	85

Mcleod v Commissioner of Police for the Metropolis 1994	166
McNaughton 1843	150
Miller 1954	75
Mitchell 1983	77
National Coal Board v Gamble 1959 1 QB 11	146
Oxford v Moss 1979	131
Pagett 1983 76 CR App R 279	48
Pearson 1992 Crim LR 193	68
Pitham and Hehl 1977 65 Cr App R 45	104
Pitwood 1902 19 TLR 37	51
Prince 1875	58
Rance v Mid-Downs Health Authority 1991 1 QB 587	64
Re A (Children) 2000 EWCA Civ 254	154
R V G 2009	102
R v Ireland 1973	84
R v JM and Son 2012	76
R v M and Another 2009	61
R v R 1992	96
R v Watson 2015	96
R v Wood Treatment Ltd 2021	79
Robinson 1979 Crim LR 173	107
Samuels v Stubbs 1972	112
Savage 1991	83
Scott v Shepherd 1773 2 Wm Bl 892	84
Smith v Chief Superintendent of Woking Police Station 1983	82
Smith 1974 QB 354	113
Smith and Morgan 2000 UKHL 49 AC 146	69
Steer 1988 AC 111	111
Stevens v Gurley 1859 7 CB NS 99	110
Sweet v Parsley 1970 AC 132	59
Tuck v Robson 1970 1 WLR 741	144
Wacker 2003 EWCA Crim 1944 4 AlL ER 295	78

White 1910	49
Whoolley 1997	150
Wilcox v Jeffrey 1951 1 ALL ER 464	144
Williams 1992 1 WLR 380 2 ALL ER 183	66
Williams (Gladstone) 1987 3 ALL ER 411 78 Cr App R 276	153
Willer 1986 83 CR App R 225	155
Wilson 1955 1 WLR 493	82
Winzar v Chief Constable of Kent 1983	47
Woollin 1998 UKHL 28	54
Woolmington v DPP 1935 AC 462	45

****

Introduction

This Revised edition of the latest book in the *Emerald Home Lawyer Series* is a companion volume to Emerald Guide to The English Legal System. The law is up to date to **2023**. All updates are included such as the recently passed Online Safety Bill that is set to become law in 2023. In addition, there are two new chapters on Cyber Crime and Animal Welfare.

An outline of the operation of the court system in Scotland and Northern Ireland is also included in Chapter one.

With the United Kingdom having departed the European Union (from January 1, 2021) there have been changes in the legal system and the hierarchy of Courts within the UK. Correspondingly, the hierarchy of courts involved in criminal cases has changed, i.e., the role of the European Courts changed although have not disappeared immediately. This is discussed more fully in Chapter 1.

Current problems with the Criminal Justice System

The pandemic intensified the problems in England and Wales' chronically under-funded justice system. Over the past decade the Ministry of Justice has suffered deeper cuts than any other Whitehall department – losing more than a quarter of its budget. Covid exposed fresh cracks in the structure of the justice system.

By contrast, courts hosting only lawyer versus lawyer exchanges adapted remarkably smoothly to remote video working. What exasperates many solicitors, barristers and judges in the criminal justice system is that hundreds of court buildings were sold off at a time when cuts to police and prosecutors may have temporarily depressed crime figures.

Entitlement thresholds for legal aid in criminal cases have not been updated for years meaning the number of unrepresented defendants is growing. Fees for legal aid cases, after years of being frozen, have grudgingly been raised a little. Criminal solicitors are abandoning the profession because it is no longer profitable. Funding is at the root of many of the justice system's problems.

In 2022, thousands of Barristers took part in a strike over the fees for criminal work. This prompted the government to offer more money as the strike was causing a paralysis in the legal system.

This book commences with the development of law generally, as to understand the context within which criminal law operates, it is first necessary to understand the workings of the legal system. Following this, the purpose of criminal law is outlined, along with an examination of areas of criminal law, such as unlawful killing, specifically murder and manslaughter. The area of non-fatal offences against the person is examined along with property offences and obtaining property by deception. Sexual offences and fraud are also included.

The areas of criminal damage and defences generally in criminal cases are outlined along with inchoate offences. Finally, the book looks at the legal system and how it operates on a day-to-day basis when hearing criminal cases.

Overall, this introduction to criminal law is wide ranging and is illustrated throughout with relevant cases. The book will prove invaluable either as a student handbook or as a guide for the professional or layperson who wishes to enhance their knowledge of criminal law.

Chapter 1

The Development of Law

The law in England and Wales has developed gradually over time. Law has been developed in a number of different ways, and the methods of developing law are known as *sources* of law. Historically, the most important ways were custom and decisions of judges. Parliament became more powerful in the eighteenth and nineteenth centuries, with Acts of Parliament becoming the main source of new laws, although judicial decisions were, and are, still important.

During the twentieth century, statute law and judicial decisions continued to be the main sources of law, but increasingly two new sources of law became important: delegated legislation and European legislation. Together, all these sources of law have combined to create the present-day legal system. However, as we have discussed in the introduction, the landscape has changed considerably since the United Kingdom departed the European Union on 1st January 2021.

Customs

Customs are rules of behaviour which develop in a community. There are two main types of custom: general and local customs.

General customs

General customs are common customs that have developed and have been absorbed over time into law.

Local customs
Local customs is a term used where a person claims that he or she is entitled to some local right, such as a right of way or the right to use land in a certain way, because this is what has happened locally over time. Judges have a test of what constitutes local customs. These are as follows:
- The custom must have existed since 'time immemorial'.
- The custom must have been exercised peaceably openly and as of right.
- The custom must be definite as to locality, nature and scope.
- The custom must be reasonable.

It is very rare for a new custom to be considered by courts nowadays. There have been certain exceptions. For example, in *Egerton v Harding (1974)* the court decided that there was a customary duty to fence land against cattle straying from the common. Although customs develop they are not part of the law until recognised by the courts.

Common law
The legal system historically could not rely on customs alone. In Anglo-Saxon times there were local courts that decided disputes but it was not until after the Norman Conquest in 1066 that a more organised system of courts developed. Norman kings realised that control of the country was that much easier if the legal system was also controlled. William the Conqueror set up the Curia Regis (The Kings Court) and appointed judges to hear disputes from the nobles. In addition to this central court, judges were sent to major towns to decide important cases.

In the time of Henry 11 (1154-89) these tours became more regular and the country was divided up into circuits, or areas for the judges to visit. Initially the judges would use the local customs or the old Anglo-Saxon laws to decide cases. On return to London the judges would discuss customs and gradually these evolved into a uniform or common law.

Common law is the basis of our law today, an unwritten law that developed from customs and judicial decisions. The phrase 'common law' is still used to distinguish laws that have been developed by judicial decisions, from laws that have been created by statute or other legislation. For example, murder is a common law crime whilst theft is a statutory crime.

Common law also has another meaning. It is used to distinguish between rules that were developed by the common law courts (the Kings Courts) and the rules of equity which were developed by the Lord Chancellor and the Chancery Courts.

Equity

Historically this is an important source still playing a part today with many of our legal concepts having developed from equitable principles. The word 'equity' has a meaning of fairness and this is the basis on which it operates.

Equity developed because of problems in the common law. Only certain types of cases were recognised. The law was also very technical; if there was an error in the formalities, the person making the claim would lose the case. People who could not obtain justice in the common law courts appealed to the King. Most of these cases were referred to the Kings Chancellor. This was because the Chancellor based his decisions on principles of natural justice and fairness, deciding on what seemed right in a particular case as opposed to the strict following of previous precedents. Account was also taken of what the parties had originally intended.

To ensure that decisions were fair, new procedures were introduced such as subpoenas, which ordered a witness to attend court. New remedies for compensation were developed which were able to compensate plaintiffs more fully than those previously used. The main equitable remedies were injunctions, specific performance; rescission and rectification. These are all still in use today and will be explained more fully later in this book.

Judicial precedents
The doctrine of precedents

Judicial precedent refers to the source of law where decisions of judges in the past create law for future judges to follow. This source of law is also known as case law and is a major source of law. The English system of precedent is based on the Latin maxim *stare decisis et non quieta movere* which is usually shortened to *stare decisis* and which translated means 'stand by what has been decided and do not unsettle the established'. This supports the idea of fairness and certainty in law.

Ratio Decidendi

Precedent is only relevant and can only be effective if the reasons for past decisions are known. Judges will outline reasons for decisions and the rationale for a judgement outlining the principles of law used. These principles are an important part of any judgement and are known as the *ratio decidendi* which means the reason for deciding. This is what creates the precedent for future judges to follow.

Obiter Dicta
The remainder of the judgement is called *obiter dicta* (other things said) and judges in future cases do not have to follow it.

Original precedent
If the point of law in a case has never been decided before, then whatever the judge decides will form a new precedent for future cases to follow. As there are no past cases for a judge to base his decision on, he is likely to look at cases which are the closest in principle and he may decide to use similar rules. This way of arriving at a judgement is called reasoning by analogy. The idea of creating new law by analogy can be seen in *Hunter and others v Canary Wharf Limited and London Docklands Development Corporation (1995)*. Part of the decision involved whether the interference with television reception could constitute an actionable private nuisance. The facts of the case were that the main tower Canary Wharf built in the Isle of Dogs East London, was 250 metres high and 50 metres square. The claimant and others claimed damages from the defendant for continuing interference over a number of years with the television reception in the area because of the height of the tower. In the Court of Appeal, the Lord Justice Pill stated:

'Lord Irving (counsel for the defendants) submits that interference with television reception by reason of the presence of a building is properly to be regarded as analogous to loss of aspect (view). To obstruct the receipt of television signals by the

erection of a building between the point of receipt and the source is not in law a nuisance............... I accept the importance of television in the lives of people. However, in my judgement the erection or presence of a building in the line of sight between a television transmitter and other properties is not actionable as an interference with the use and enjoyment of land. The analogy with loss of prospect is compelling. The loss of a view, which may be of the greatest importance to householders, is not actionable and neither is the mere presence of a building in the site lines to the television transmitter'.

Binding precedent

This is a precedent from an earlier case which must be followed even if the judge in the later case does not agree with the principle. A binding precedent is only created where the facts of the second case are sufficiently similar to the original case.

Persuasive precedent

This is a precedent that is not binding on the court but the judge may consider it and decide that it is a correct principle and is persuaded that it should be followed.

Persuasive precedent comes from a number of sources:

- Courts lower in the hierarchy.
- Decisions by the Judicial Committee of the Privy Council.
- Statements made obiter dicta.
- A dissenting judgement.
- Decisions of courts in foreign countries.

The hierarchy of courts and precedent-England and Wales

In England and Wales courts operate a rigid hierarchy of judicial precedents. Every court is bound to follow any decision made by a court above it in the hierarchy. In general, appellate courts (appeal courts) are bound by their own decisions. The diagram below indicates the hierarchy of criminal courts.

CRIMINAL COURTS IN ENGLAND AND WALES
UK Supreme Court   Appeal only, on points of law   Justices of the Supreme Court
Court of Appeal   Appeal only, on points of law to either   the Criminal or Civil Divisions: Lord Chief Justice,   Heads of Division and   Court of Appeal judges
High Court   Chancery, Queen's Bench and Family Divisions. All three divisions hear appeals from other courts, as well as "first instance" cases.   High Court and Deputy High Court Judges
Crown Court   Jury trial for all indictable and some either-way criminal offences. Appeals against conviction and sentence from the magistrates' court.   Circuit judges, Recorders and jury
Magistrates' Court   Trial for most criminal offences. Some civil matters.   Magistrates, District Judges   (Magistrates' Courts), Deputy DJ (MC)

The European Court of Justice and BREXIT

The Court of Justice of the EU (CJEU) interprets EU law. Its purpose is to ensure the uniform application of EU law across all Member States. The UK is no longer a member of the EU, but the CJEU will continue to play a role in UK law.

Under the Withdrawal Act (WA) 2020 the CJEU's jurisdiction continues beyond the transition period in some areas. First, its jurisdiction over concepts of EU law that arise over the interpretation and application of the WA lasts as long as aspects of the WA remain in operation. In the case of Part 2 of the WA on citizens' rights, this is as long as EU citizens and UK nationals covered by Part 2 remain alive. In the case of the Protocol on Ireland/Northern Ireland, the CJEU's jurisdiction could be indefinite.

Article 86(1) of the WA makes it clear that any cases pending before the CJEU at the end of the transition period will fall within the CJEU's jurisdiction until they are finalised. This includes decisions on appeals.

Article 87 of the WA adds to this more specifically. It states that the European Commission has four years from the end of the transition period to bring infringement proceedings against the UK for breaches of EU law that took place during the transition period.

Any judgment handed down by the CJEU that is covered by these provisions will remain binding on the UK. As such, it is possible that a proceeding commenced by the European Commission in 2024 about a UK action (or failure to act) in 2020 will be decided by the CJEU in 2025 and will be binding on the UK.

The Supreme Court
Form 1st October 2009, The Supreme Court of the United Kingdom assumed jurisdiction on points of law for all civil cases in the UK and criminal cases in England and Wales and Northern Ireland.

Court of appeal
The court of appeal is next in the hierarchy and has two divisions, civil and criminal. Both divisions are bound to follow the decisions of the Supreme Court. They must also follow past decisions of their own although there are exceptions to the rule and the Court of Appeal (Criminal Division) is more flexible where it involves the liberty of the subject.

Divisional courts
The three divisional courts, Queens Bench, Chancery and Family are bound by the House of Lords and the Court of Appeal. The divisional courts are also bound by their own past decisions, although there are some exceptions.

Courts of first instance
This term means any court where the original trial of a case is held. Appeal courts do not hear any original trials only appeals from those trials. Courts of first instance rarely ever create precedents only following decisions of courts above them.

The High Court
The High Court is bound by decisions of all courts above it and in turn it binds the lower courts.

Inferior courts

Inferior courts are the Crown Court, the County Court and the Magistrates Court. They are bound to follow decisions of all higher courts. It is very unlikely that a decision by a lower court can create a precedent. The one exception is that a ruling on a point of law by a judge in a Crown Court will bind the Magistrates Court.

Use of Practice Statement

Since 1966 the Practice Statement has allowed the House of Lords to change the law if it believes that an earlier case was wrongly decided. It does not affect the precedential value of cases in lower courts; all other courts that recognise the Supreme Court as the court of last resort are still bound by Supreme Court decisions. Before this, the only way a binding precedent could be avoided was to create new legislation on the matter.

Distinguishing, overruling and reversing previous decisions

Distinguishing is a method used by a judge to avoid following a past decision which otherwise would have to be followed. It means that the judge finds that the material facts of the case he/she is following are sufficiently different for him to draw a distinction between the present case and the previous case. He/she is not then bound by the previous case.

Overruling is where a court in a later case decides that the legal rule in a previous case is wrong. Overruling may occur when a higher court overrules a decision by a lower court, for example the Supreme Court overruling a decision by the Court of Appeal. Reversing is where a court higher up in the hierarchy overturns the decision of a lower court on appeal in the same case.

Advantages and disadvantages of precedent in the law

There are advantages and disadvantages to the way judicial precedent operates in England and Wales. The main advantages to the operation of precedent are:

Certainty-Because the courts follow past decisions, people know what the law is and how it is likely to be applied in their case. Lawyers advise clients on the likely outcome of cases and it also allows people to operate their businesses in the certainty that what they do is within the law.

Consistency and fairness-It is seen as just and fair that similar cases are decided in the same way.

Precision-As the principles of law are set out in actual cases, the law becomes very precise.

Flexibility-There is room for the law to change as the House of Lords can use the Practice Statement to overrule cases.

Time- saving-Precedent can be considered a useful time saving device as where a principle has been established, cases with similar facts are unlikely to go through the lengthy process of litigation.

Disadvantages

Rigidity-The fact that lower courts must follow decisions of higher courts, together with the fact that the Court of Appeal has to follow its own past decisions, can make the law too inflexible so that bad decisions made in the past can be perpetuated.

Complexity-There are many reported cases and it may be complex and time consuming to find the right case on which to base a decision.

Illogical distinction-The use of distinguishing to avoid past decisions can lead to illogical distinctions so that some areas of law have become very complex.

The Hierarchy of Courts in Scotland

The administration of justice in Scotland is the responsibility of the civil, criminal and heraldic courts of the country. In Scotland, courts are divided on the cases of the types of cases they hear and these include civil and criminal. The Court of Session is the Supreme Civil Court in the country whereas the High Court of Justiciary is the Supreme Criminal Court.

There is a hierarchy structure followed within each brand of the judicial system of Scotland.

Civil Courts

The Supreme Court of the United Kingdom

This is the highest civil court of appeal for Scotland and hears appeals from all civil courts of the UK and the criminal, civil courts of England and Wales and Northern Ireland.

Court of Session

This is the Supreme Civil court which ranks 2nd on the hierarchy of Civil courts in Scotland and is both court of appeal as well as that of the first instance. The first instance court is called the Outer house and the appeal court is known as the Inner House.

Sheriff Court
This is the 3rd level civil court in Scotland which sits locally. A number of high value cases or the difficult cases in the country are brought in the sessions court.

Criminal Courts
High Court of Justiciary
This is the supreme or the main criminal court in Scotland and is both a court of appeal as well as that of appeal. There is no other petition or appeal from the High court's decision.

District Court
Each district court is composed of either one or more of Justices of Peace who either sit alone or in groups of 3s with a qualified or capable UK legal system assessor. District courts handle those kinds of cases that are related to violation of the peace, minor assaults, offences, petty theft, and drunkenness etc.

Justice of the Peace Courts
Justice of the Peace Courts also known as JP courts) are a unique part of Scotland's criminal justice system. A justice of the peace is a lay magistrate, appointed from within the local community and trained in criminal law and procedure. Justices sit either alone, or in a bench of three, and deal with the less serious summary crimes, such as speeding, careless driving and breach of the peace. In court justices have access to advice on the law and procedure from lawyers, who fulfil the role of legal advisers or clerk of court.

Justice of the peace courts have replaced the district courts that were established in 1975 under local authority administration. The justice of the peace courts are administered, along with the other courts, by the Scottish Courts and Tribunals Service.

Tribunals and Special Courts:
Scotland has several tribunals or special courts: The Tribunals preside in judgement over several types of specialist areas. some of the tribunals are:
- Employment tribunal
- Asylum and immigration tribunal
- Mental health tribunal for Scotland
- VAT and duties tribunal
- Pensions Appeal Tribunals for Scotland
- Children's hearings
- Court of the Lord Lyon
- Court martial
- General assembly of the church of Scotland

See overleaf for the Hierarchy of Courts in Scotland.

HIERARCHY OF COURTS IN SCOTLAND

CIVIL COURT

THE SUPREME COURT OF THE UNITED KINGDOM
|
COURT OF SESSION
|
SHERIFF COURT

CRIMINAL COURTS

HIGH COURT OF JUSTICIARY
|
SHERIFF COURT
|
DISTRICT COURT
|
JUSTICE OF THE PEACE COURTS

TRIBUNAL AND SPECIAL COURTS

TRIBUNALS
|
CHILDREN'S HEARING'S
|
COURT OF THE LORD LYON
|
COURT MARTIAL
|
GENERAL ASSEMBLY OF THE CHURCH OF SCOTLAND

The legal system in Northern Ireland

Northern Ireland has its own judicial system which is headed by the Lord Chief Justice of Northern Ireland.

The Department of Justice is responsible for the administration of the courts, which it runs through the Northern Ireland Courts and Tribunals Service. The Department also has responsibility for policy and legislation about criminal law, legal aid policy, the police, prisons and probation.

In both criminal and civil cases, the courts make decisions on an adversarial rather than an inquisitorial basis. This means that both sides test the credibility and reliability of the evidence their opponent presents to the court. The judge or jury makes decisions based on the evidence presented.

Courts In Northern Ireland

UK Supreme Court	Hears appeals on points of law in cases of major public importance
The Court of Appeal	Hears appeals on points of law in criminal and civil cases from all courts
The High Court	Hears complex or important civil cases and appeals from county court
The Crown Court	Hears all serious criminal cases
Magistrates Court (Including Youth Courts and Family Proceedings	Hears less serious criminal cases, cases involving juveniles and civil and family cases.
The Enforcements of Judgements Office	Enforces civil judgements

Agencies involved in the justice system

The justice system in Northern Ireland is made up of a number of agencies who are responsible for the administration of justice, maintaining law and order, detecting and stopping crime, dealing with offenders and overseeing the work of prisons.
- Police Service of Northern Ireland
- Public Prosecution Service
- Northern Ireland Courts and Tribunals Service
- Northern Ireland Prison Service
- Probation Board for Northern Ireland
- Forensic Science Northern Ireland
- Criminal Justice Inspection Northern Ireland
- Youth Justice Agency

Reporting cases England and Wales, Scotland and Northern Ireland

Written law reports have existed in England and Wales since the 13th century. Reports right from the early times were inaccurate and difficult to follow. In 1865 the Incorporated Council of Law was set up, controlled by the courts. Law reports became more accurate and precise, with judgements being noted word for word. This accuracy of reports was one of the factors in the development of the strict doctrine of precedent. There are also other well-established reports today, notably the All-England Series (abbreviated to All ER) and the weekly law Reports (WLR). The internet also provides reports, websites such as:
- www.lawreports.co.uk and www.publications.parliament.uk.
- In Scotland the Scottish Council of Law Reporting undertakes responsibility of reporting of legal cases.

- The Northern Ireland Law Reports is the official series of law reports for Northern Ireland which covers cases decided in the Superior Courts in Northern Ireland and on appeal from in the Supreme Court.

****

Chapter 2

The Purpose of Criminal Law

Having looked at the development of law and the operations and structure of the legal system(s) we will now turn to criminal law generally. The main purposes of criminal law are to:

- Protect individuals and their property from damage or harm.
- To preserve order in society.
- To punish those who deserve punishment.

The most important distinction between civil law and criminal law is that, under criminal law, with which this book deals, the state plays a major role. Criminal law is, in effect, a crime against the state.

Defining a crime

There are varying definitions of a crime but they are all variations on the same theme. Essentially a crime is:

- A conduct forbidden by the state. Punishment is meted out to any person who violates the rules of criminal law. The state enforces those rules.

It is true to say that many offences committed involve breaches of morals, or moral wrongs. However, there are many subtle differences between morality and crime. There are areas of morality which are not crimes, moral wrongs such as adultery or telling of lies. Although these kinds of moral wrongs are offensive to many people the law would not get involved.

The Wolfenden Committee of 1957 concluded that it is not the function of criminal law to interfere with the private lives of citizens in order to try to impose certain standards of behaviour. It was felt that this should only be done:

"To preserve public order and decency to protect the citizen from what is offensive or injurious, and to provide sufficient safeguards against exploitation and corruption of others, particularly those who are especially vulnerable".

Sources of criminal law

Criminal law combines a mix of common law rules and Acts of Parliament. Common law rules are rules that have been laid down over time by judges. However, Parliament is now the dominating law-making assembly. The sources of criminal law are therefore mixed.

The crimes of murder and manslaughter provide an example of the interaction between the judiciary and Parliament. Until the middle of this century, until the 1965 Murder (Abolition of Death Penalty) Act, murder was punishable by death. After 1965 the death penalty was abolished except for murder or treason (it was finally abolished in Northern Ireland in 1973). The Crime and Disorder Act 1998 removed the death penalty for treason and piracy. There is no Act of Parliament that defines murder. This has been developed by the judiciary over the years. Their definition originally stated that death had to occur within a year and a day. In 1996, this definition was abolished with the passing of the Law Reform (Year and a Day Rule) Act 1996. In regard to voluntary manslaughter, this was originally curtailed by the judges.

The classification of offences

Offences can be divided into summary offences and indictable offences. Summary offences are more minor offences and indictable more serious. There is a third category that fits in between the former two, triable either way offences.

Summary offences

These offences must first be tried in a Magistrates Court. They are usually always dealt with there and then by magistrates and do not progress to Crown Court. Such cases are:
- Speeding and careless driving
- Minor criminal damage
- Assault and battery
- Assaulting a police officer in the course of his duty
- Drunken driving

Indictable offences

These are more serious or complicated cases that cannot be decided by magistrates. They will be dealt with by the Crown Court. These offences include:
- Rape
- Murder
- Manslaughter
- Robbery
- Arson

The magistrates will decide whether the defendant is remanded on bail or is held in custody. The Bail Act 1976 states that everyone has a general right to bail unless the offence is particularly serious, such as violence or sexual offences. Magistrates must justify their reasoning.

Bail and the Policing and Crime Act 2017
It was intended that the Act, which became law on 31st January 2017, should improve decision making and reduce distress and injustice for individuals placed on bail. Accordingly, On Monday 3rd April 2017, The Policing and Crime Act made it a legal requirement for the police to limit the pre-charge bail period to 28 days.

BAIL – The Criminal Procedure (Amendment) Rules 2023
The CPAR Rules 2023 have significantly modified the process of bail and the Police and Crime Act 2017.

As we have seen pre-charge bail (also known as police bail) is a process by which a person is released from custody after being arrested pending further investigation – whilst also possibly being subject to certain bail conditions. They are required to return to the police station at a specified date/time whereby they are given an update on their case. At this point, they may be charged, have their bail extended, be Released Under Investigation (RUI), or be released with No Further Action (NFA).

The Government legislated through the Policing and Crime Act 2017 to address concerns that individuals were being kept on pre-charge bail for lengthy periods. The reforms introduced a 'presumption' against pre-charge bail unless it is necessary and proportionate in all circumstances. They also brought about clear statutory timescales and processes for the initial imposition and extension of bail, including the introduction of judicial oversight for the extension of pre-charge bail beyond 3 months.

After these reforms came into force in April 2017, the use of pre-charge bail fell – this was reflected by an increasing number of individuals who were RUI'd. This raised concerns that pre-charge bail was not always being used where it might have been appropriate.

The Criminal Procedure (Amendment) Rules 2023 (CPAR 2023) have now brought about significant changes to the way that pre-charge bail is managed.

These reforms have been brought about for a multitude of reasons. A major driving force is to dissuade the use of RUI which has been subject to criticism since its introduction in 2017. This was partly in response to the murder of Kay Richardson, who was killed by her ex-partner while he was RUI and not subjected to bail conditions.

Building on this, another downside to RUI is that many people have been RUI'd for lengthy periods – sometimes for over a year – without knowing anything about the status of their investigation. It can be argued that being RUI leaves people in an unfair 'legal limbo' where they don't quite know where they stand for extended periods of time.

The new system

The CPAR 2023 has modified how pre-charge bail works. Sections 47ZA and 47ZB of the Police and Criminal Evidence Act 1984 limit the period for which a person may be subject to pre-charge bail. This period may be extended in specific circumstances by a senior police officer/Court. This was overhauled in 2020 by the Police, Crime, Sentencing and Courts Act 2022 which lengthened the time period for which people can be subject to pre-charge bail.

Additionally, pre-charge bail can also be extended by police officers of rank inspector and above for up to 6 months, and extended by officers of rank superintendents or above by up to 9 months:

"Under sections 47ZC and 47ZD of the 1984 Act, in a standard case the applicable bail period may be extended on the authority of a police officer of the rank of inspector or above until the end of 6 months from the bail start date. Under section 47ZDA the applicable bail period may be further extended on the authority of a police officer of the rank of superintendent or above until the end of 9 months from the bail start date."

Building on the above, the CPAR 2023 has now further extended the period to which a person can be kept on pre-charge bail by a Magistrates' Court (and others). They replaced all references to '12 months' in The Criminal Procedure Rules 2020 to '24 months', such that it now states:

"Under section 47ZF of the 1984 Act, on an application made before the date on which the applicable bail period ends by a constable, a member of staff of the FCA of the description designated by its Chief Executive, an officer of Revenue and Customs, an NCA officer, a member of the SFO or a Crown Prosecutor, a Magistrates' Court may authorize an extension of that period –

- *(a) from a previous total of 9 months to a new total of 12 months or, if the investigation is unlikely to be completed or a police charging decision made within a lesser period, a new total of 18 months (following extension under section 47ZDA of the Act);*
- *(b) from a previous total of 12 months to a new total of 18 months or, if the investigation is unlikely to be completed or a police charging decision made within a lesser period, a new total of **24 months** (following extension under section 47ZDB or 47ZE of the Act)."*

For the reasons mentioned above, a major function of the newly introduced CPAR 2023 is that it will promote the use of pre-charge bail as opposed to RUI, due to the fact that pre-charge bail can now be in effect for longer periods, i.e., up to 24 months. It can also be extended purely by the prerogative of inspectors/superintendents and above, as mentioned above. Under previous rules, the police could only release a person on pre-charge bail for up to 3 months – any extension beyond this period required judicial oversight via an application made to the Magistrates' Court.

One concern is that the police now have a greater deal of control over an individual's liberty before they have even been formally charged with a crime. On the other hand, the new rules are expected to have multifaceted benefits. For instance, upon release from custody, people will have much more clarity regarding their case moving forward; pre-charge bail involves firm deadlines so that people know how long they are on bail for and ensures that they are informed about the status of their case. Additionally, the timeframes set on pre-charge bail may encourage the police to work more expeditiously than if the individual was RUI'd (which has no set deadline). Another view is that it would provide additional safety measures to potential complainants through the use of bail conditions.

Triable either-way offences
These offences may be tried either summarily or by indictment. If the magistrates decide that it is serious enough to be tried in a Crown Court then the defendant has no say in the matter of where it is tried. However, if the magistrates decide that they can try the case then the defendant can decide whether he wants it tried in the Magistrates Court or whether it should go to Crown Court. If the defendant decides on a Magistrates Court trial, then he will be warned that the case could still go to the Crown Court. Examples of triable either-way offences include:

- Dangerous driving
- Obtaining property or services by deception
- Theft
- Burglary
- Criminal damage over £5,000

Elements of a crime
The burden of proof in criminal law
In all cases, before a person can be convicted of a wrong against the State, the jury must be convinced by the prosecution that he has committed the crime of which he is accused. The prosecution must establish the burden of proof beyond all reasonable doubt.

One case that clarified this was *Woolmington v DPP 1935*. In this case, the defendant claimed that he took a gun with him to the home of the victim's mother, with no criminal intention, but to demonstrate to his estranged wife that he planned to commit suicide if she didn't return to him. The gun, so the defendant alleged, went off by accident and he shot his estranged wife and was convicted of murder.

The House of Lords overturned the judgement on appeal stating that it was not necessary for the defendant to prove his innocence and that the shooting was accidental, but for the prosecution to prove guilt by establishing that the killing had been intentional.

Establishing criminal liability

The prosecution in a case, when trying to establish criminal liability, will usually have to prove several things:
- that the defendant has actually committed the crime in question. This is known as the *actus reus* of the offence.
- that the defendant had committed the wrong with the degree of blameworthiness required by the law, with the necessary 'guilty mind'. This element of the offence is known as the *mens rea.*

The *actus reus* of a crime

The establishment of *actus reus* or the existence of *actus reus* is essential for criminal liability to be proven. At the most basic level, the actus rea of an offence will consist of an act or physical element. Each crime has its own *actus reus,* laid down either by judges or statute. An *actus reus* of theft, for example, under the Theft Act 1968, arises where a party 'appropriates property belonging to another'. In the offence of battery, the physical element is the use of unlawful force.

Some crimes require the production of consequences as a result of the action (result crimes). For example, in murder the actus reus requires both conduct on the part of the accused (physical element) and death of the victim (consequence). In many cases, the actions and motivations of the accused will be plain to see but others can be more complex.

State of affairs cases

Some unusual cases cannot be discussed in terms of acts and are often referred to as "state of affairs" cases. These are cases where the actus reus consists of circumstances and sometimes consequences but no acts, i.e., "being" rather than "doing" offences.

In *Winzar v Chief Constable of Kent (1983)* D was convicted of "being found drunk on a highway" contrary to s.12 of the Licensing Acts 1872. The police had found D drunk in a hospital and removed him from the premises, subsequently leaving him on a highway in the same state. This conviction was upheld on appeal despite the fact that D was not responsible for being placed on the highway in the first place.

Conduct of the accused

In many cases, the conduct of the accused may be enough to show the *actus reus* has been committed. A clear case of this is perjury or lying under oath. Another example is theft. Once a person has taken property belonging to someone else, the *actus reus* of the offence will have been established.

If the accused has done this intentionally then it will be deemed that he will also have the necessary guilty mind.

Result or consequence
As we have seen, for the commission of some crimes it is necessary to demonstrate the result or consequence of the crime as well as conduct. For example, in the crime of murder, the violent act must have resulted in an unlawful killing.

Causation
One aspect of a*ctus reus* is causation. Causation must be established for nearly all offences. However, the crime of murder provides the best illustrations of the operations of the principles involved. Whether a defendant's acts or omissions caused the victim's death is always for the jury to decide. The judge should always direct them as to the elements of causation, but it is for them to decide if the causal link between the defendant's act and the consequences has been established. Usually, it will be sufficient to direct a jury 'simply that in law the accuseds act need not be the sole cause, or even the main cause of the victim's death, it being enough that his act contributed significantly to that result' *(R. V Pagett 1983)*. In this case, several police officers were trying to arrest the defendant for several serious offences. He was hiding in the first floor flat with his pregnant girlfriend, Gail Kinchen. The defendant armed himself with a shotgun and, against her will, used Gail's body to shield himself as he tried to escape. He fired at two officers, who returned fire. Three bullets fired by the police officers hit and killed Gail. The defendant was convicted of manslaughter.

The Court of Appeal dismissed his appeal. In this case it said that it was reasonably foreseeable that the police would return fire in self-defence or in the lawful exercise of their duty.

Factual causation
The defendant's conduct must be a factual cause of the consequences. This is commonly applied using the 'but for' test. In other words, it must be established that the consequences would not have occurred as and when it did but for the defendant's conduct. One case highlighting this is *R v White 1910*, where White put potassium cyanide into his mother's drink in order to kill her, so that he could gain under her will. His mother was found dead with a glass of the poisoned drink beside her. However, medical evidence established that she died of a heart attack, not poisoning. White had not used enough cyanide to kill his mother. He was acquitted of murder but convicted of the attempt.

Legal causation
This is closely associated with moral responsibility. The question is whether the result can be fairly said to be the fault of the defendant. In *Marchant and Muntz (2004)* Edward Muntz, a Warwickshire farmer, owned a Matbro TR250 loading machine, an agricultural vehicle with a grab attached at the front for lifting and moving large hay bales. The grab consisted of nine spikes (called tynes) each one metre in length. Muntz gave instructions to an employee, Tom Marchant to take the vehicle onto a public road to deliver some hay bales. Marchant stopped, waiting to make a turn onto a farm track when Richard Fletcher, a motorcyclist approached at high speed from the opposite direction, collided with the vehicle and was impaled on one of the tynes and later died. Muntz and Marchant were convicted respectively of causing death by dangerous driving and procuring the offence, but the Court of Appeal quashed their convictions.

Expert evidence at the trial indicated that the tyne could have been covered by some sort of guard, but Grigson J concluded that, even had such a guard been in place it would not have prevented a probable fatal collision.

The acceleration principle
The defendant's act will be considered a cause if it has accelerated the victim's death. In addition, other causes may be the actions of third parties or the actions of the victim himself.

An omission
In English law a person will not be found to be criminally liable merely because he has failed to act. This was outlined in the nineteenth century by Stephen LJ when he stated:

It is not a crime to cause death or bodily injury, even intentionally, by any omission.

Stephen L J went on to describe a situation where a person sees another person drowning but does not reach out to help him, although by doing so this would have saved the person life. This is not a crime. There are a few exceptions to the rule. They include the following situations:

- gangrene in her leg and died and a limited number of statutory provisions create liability for omissions. Under the Road Traffic Act 1988, a person failing to provide a breath test as required is liable as is someone failing to give details to someone entitled to receive them after a road traffic accident and someone failing to report an accident as required. It is also a statutory offence to fail to provide a child with adequate food, shelter, or medical help, under the Children's and Young Person's Act 1933.

- Where there is a contractual duty to act in a certain way. There may be a duty under a contract to behave in a specific way. One such case demonstrating this was *R. V Pittwood 1902* where an employee was employed to guard a level crossing. The guard opened a gate to allow a cart through but failed to close the gate. A few minutes later, a passing train hit a hay cart crossing the track killing the cart driver.
- Where there is a duty imposed by law. The judges have imposed liability for omissions in certain situations and circumstances. In *R.V Dytham 1979*, a police officer stood by and watched a man being kicked to death. The Court of Appeal upheld the criminal conviction for misconduct in a public offence. A party may also be found guilty of failing to act if there is a duty imposed on him by virtue of the special relationship between him and the victim. One such case was *R. V Instan 1893* where a niece failed to get help for her aunt with whom she was living. The aunt contracted the niece was held guilty of manslaughter. Two other areas where omission implies liability are where the defendant has voluntarily accepted responsibility for the other and where there is liability under a continuous act.

The *Mens Rea* of a crime

As seen, many cases require a physical element, the actus reus and a mental element, the mens rea. In most cases it will be necessary that the defendant has committed the act with the relevant *mens rea* or the degree of blameworthiness required by the offence. Some offences, such as the offence of strict liability, outlined later do not require fault to be proved. *Mens Rea* means the mental element, or state of mind, that the defendant must possess at the time of performing whatever crime he or she is involved in.

Different degrees of *mens rea*
This varies depending on the seriousness of the offence. In the most serious criminal offences, the prosecution will usually have to prove a high degree of blameworthiness. The defendant will only be held to be guilty if it can be proved that he fully intended to commit the crime.

Crimes of specific intent
Murder is a crime of specific intent where the accused will only be convicted by the jury if they are convinced that he meant to kill or cause grievous bodily harm. Intention is also needed for theft crimes. The accused will not be convicted unless it can be demonstrated that he took property with the intention of permanently depriving the other person of it.

Crime of basic intent
There are certain crimes that do not require such a high degree of fault to be demonstrated. They can be committed either with intention or recklessly. Such offences are assault, battery, actual bodily harm and malicious wounding.

Intention
A jury must decide whether the accused carried out a crime with intent. There is no clear definition of intention. They can only arrive at this conclusion through examining all the evidence. Judges have stated that intention to do something should not be confused with the desire or motive to do something. We might

contemplate doing something but we cannot be tried for it unless we actually do it.

Cunliffe v Goodman 1950 highlighted this when it was stated that intention is a state of affairs *'that a person does more than merely contemplate'*.

The intention to commit a crime should not be confused with motivation, as this is secondary. Although the defendant might feel justified in acting as he did. However, the fact that intention exists means that the *mens rea* will have been established. The motive is irrelevant.

Direct intention
Direct intent is where the consequence is desired and the accused decides to bring it about. In a lot of cases, it will not be difficult for the jurors to decide whether the defendant had the required *mens rea* as the circumstances are obvious. One such example might be a suicide bomber whose intentions are directly obvious. If such a person survived an attack, which is highly unlikely, then a jury would not have much problem in finding the necessary intention. Another example is murder, where the accused intended to kill or cause serious harm.

Oblique intention
Also referred to indirect intent, this arises where the intention of the offender is different to the result. This might arise for example where a person decides to cause damage to property motivated through revenge. However, when carrying out that revenge he inadvertently kills several people. This was not his intention but it happened.

The position on this is not clear and the House of Lords expressed an opinion in the case of *DPP v Smith (1961)* in which the House of Lords stated that there was an irrebutable presumption that an accused foresaw and intended any "natural consequences" of his action and that the test for determining what was a natural consequence was a purely objective one. This was reversed by the Criminal Justice Act 1967 s.8 which states that in determining whether a person has committed an offence, a court or jury shall not be bound to infer that a result was intended or foreseen only where it is a "natural and probable" consequence of these actions.

The leading case is now that of *R.V Woollin 1998*. In this case, D lost his temper and threw his three-month-old son on to a hard surface, killing him. The judges quashed the conviction and substituted murder for manslaughter. The Law Lords stated that it was clearly the jury's task to determine whether the defendant intended to kill or cause harm. In cases of oblique intent however, the jury should be directed that they are not entitled to find the necessary intention unless they feel certain that death or serious bodily harm was a virtually certain result of a defendant's action and the defendant had appreciated this fact.

Recklessness

For many offences, it is not necessary to demonstrate a high degree of blameworthiness but only to show the accused was reckless. Recklessness is the taking of unjustifiable risk. Here, we will look at two types of recklessness, or differing degrees of recklessness:

- It is argued by some that a defendant is only liable if he had actually foreseen that he was taking an unjustifiable risk. If he had not foreseen the risk then he is not liable
- The other belief is that the defendant could be convicted if he ought to have foreseen such a risk.

The types of recklessness outlined above are known respectively as Cunningham and Caldwell recklessness, so called after cases involving those named people.

Cunningham recklessness

This was established in the case of *R. V Cunningham 1957*. The action of 'malicious intent' was central to this case. The defendant stole money from a gas meter and in the process tore the meter from the wall and left the pipes exposed. Gas seeped through into next door and affected the woman residing there. Cunningham was convicted but successfully appealed. It was held that the judge had misdirected the jury by stating that 'malicious' meant 'wicked' instead of expanding on the more precise legal meaning. The Appeal Court stated that when the word 'malicious' was used in a statute, it was necessary to establish that the defendant had either intended to cause the harm in question or had foreseen that such an event would occur. Using the above as a test, Cunningham could only be convicted if he knew the risk from the gas but went on to take it nevertheless. It was not enough that he ought to have foreseen a risk. The test was subjective.

Caldwell recklessness

The above was the position until the cases of *Caldwell and Lawrence in 1982*. In Caldwell the defendant had been engaged to work for the proprietor of a hotel but was dismissed and felt a grievance against the owner. Drunk, Caldwell broke a window and started a fire on the ground floor. This was discovered and put out quickly and no harm was done with the exception of minor damage. Caldwell admitted to the charge of criminal damage but not a more serious charge of causing criminal damage with the intent to endanger life or being reckless as to whether life would be endangered. He was found guilty and given three years imprisonment. The case went to appeal, to the House of Lords, where Lord Diplock gave the main speech, changing the law on recklessness, in relation to the crime of criminal damage. He stated:

"That the only person who knows what the accused's mental processes were at the time of committing the crime is the accused himself and probably not even he can recall them accurately when the rage or excitement under which he acted has passed or he has sobered up if he were under the influence of drink at the end of the relevant time".

Lord Diplock decided that a person is reckless under the Criminal Damage Act 1971 if:

1. He does an act which in fact creates an obvious risk that property will be destroyed or damaged, and
2. when he does the act, he either has not given any thought to the possibility of there being any such risk or has recognised that there was some risk involved and has nonetheless gone on to do it.

Caldwell's appeal was dismissed and a wider test of recklessness emerged.

Negligence

Negligence occurs when a person behaves or acts in such a way that falls below the standard expected of a reasonable person in the same situation as the accused. Negligence often incurs liability in civil law but there are certain circumstances where a criminal act is also committed.

The distinction between recklessness and negligence is seen as the former being the deliberate taking of an unjustifiable risk whilst the latter is inadvertent risk taking.

Criminal negligence

Criminal negligence can be seen in dangerous driving and causing death by dangerous driving. In addition to driving offences, any grossly negligent behaviour that leads to death may result in a manslaughter charge.

Transferred malice

If a defendant has the *mens rea* for one offence, it can be transferred to another offence of the same type. One case that illustrates this is *R. V Latimer 1886* in which the defendant, a soldier, hit a customer in a pub with his belt after being attacked by the other person. The belt rebounded off the victim and hit a woman in the face wounding her. The court held that the *mens rea* from the first attack could be transferred to the other.

Strict liability

There are numerous offences, quite often of a regulatory nature, which have been created as offences of strict liability. Most have been laid out by statute but there are also common law examples such as public nuisance and libel offences. If an offence is one of strict liability, then the defendant may be held criminally liable without any proof of fault on his part. Strict liability offences require proof of the actus reus of the offence and proof that the accused persons actions were voluntary. The accused cannot claim that he took all reasonable steps to avoid committing the offence (defence of due diligence) not can he claim that he made a mistake as to the facts (defence of mistake) to avoid conviction for a strict liability offence.

An early case of strict liability without fault is that of Prince 1875. The defendant was charged under s55 Offences Against The Person Act 1861, with unlawfully taking an unmarried girl under the age of 16 out of the possession of her parents. Prince was found guilty even though the girl looked much older than her 13 years and had convinced Prince that she was 18. Liability arose when Prince committed the act.

Different types of strict liability offences-Regulatory offences

There are many of these. The case of the *London Borough of Harrow v Shah and Shah 2000* involved the defendants being charged with selling a lottery ticket to a person under 16 despite the fact that they had not been present when the transaction took place. Notices were also put up in the store. The magistrates dismissed the charge and the local authority took the case to appeal. The Divisional Court of Queen's Bench Division allowed this appeal stating that there was strict liability as the National Lottery Act 1993 and its corresponding regulations was strict and allowed no defence of 'reasonable diligence'.

More serious criminal offences

In relation to more serious offences where the outcome for the accused can be far more serious, the Supreme Court is far less ready to impose strict liability.

One case which emphasises this is *Sweet v Parsley 1970*, where a teacher leased a farmhouse near Oxford, which she then rented to students. She kept a room for her own occasional use. The students used drugs on the premises and this resulted in Sweet being convicted of being involved in the management of premises which were being used for the smoking of cannabis under the Dangerous Drugs Act 1965. The court of first instance (the originating court) and the Queens Bench Division decided that she was strictly liable. The case went to the House of Lords (now supreme Court).

Lord Reid made a clear distinction between regulatory criminal offences and ones which he decided were 'truly criminal acts'. Whereas the imposition of strict liability might well be appropriate for the former type of offence Lord Reid felt that there was a strong presumption that *mens rea* was needed for the latter type of crime. Sweet's conviction was quashed in this case. Following this case, the Dangerous Drugs Act 1965 was replaced by the Misuse of Drugs Act and the section corresponding to the one affecting Sweet was replaced by one requiring knowledge before liability is imposed.

Following on from Sweet v Parsley was the case of *Gammon (Hong Kong Ltd) v Attorney General of Hong Kong (1984)*. In this case, which involved the defendant deviating from building plans in a material way, contrary to the Hong Kong Building Ordinances the court had to decide whether it was necessary to prove that the defendant knew the deviation was material or

whether this was a strict liability matter. The Privy Council set out criteria to assist in determining whether an offence was one of strict liability. They retained the presumption in favour of mens rea for every offence but outlined situations when the presumption could be rebutted. In summary:
1) There is a presumption that mens rea is required for every statutory offence.
2) The presumption can be displaced by clear wording in a statute or by necessary implication from the effect of the statute.
3) The presumption is particularly strong where the offence is "truly criminal".
4) The only situation where the presumption can be displaced is where the statute is concerned with an issue of social concern such as public safety.
5) Even where the statute is concerned with such an issue, the presumption stands unless it can be shown that the creation of strict liability will be effective to promote the objects of the statute by encouraging greater vigilance to prevent the commission of the prohibited act.

Thus, the courts will start with a presumption in favour of mens rea but may look to the wording of the Act to determine whether the offence is one of strict liability. Words such as "knowingly" "recklessly" "permitting" or "intentionally will indicate an element of mens rea. If the particular section charged is silent on the matter, the Court will look to the rest of the Act for an indication. For example, when the section charged makes no mention of mens rea but other sections of the Act do, the offence could be considered strict liability.

The approach outlined in gammon has been followed in recent cases. In *B (a minor) v DPP (2000)* a 15-year-old boy was charged with having incited a girl under 14 to commit an act of gross indecency with him, contrary to s.1(1) of the Indecency with Children Act 1960. The House of Lords followed the approach laid down in Sweet v Parsley and, applying the usual presumption in favour of a requirement for mens rea, held that for a conviction under the section, the prosecution had to prove that the defendant was not mistaken as to the victim's age. More precisely, the prosecution had to prove an absence of genuine belief on the part of the accused, which did not have to be on reasonable grounds, that the victim was aged 14 or over. The presumption in favour of a mens rea is rebutted only if there is a compellingly clear implication that mens rea is not needed. Such an implication may be found in the language used in the wording of the offence, the nature of the offence, the mischief sought to be prevented and any other circumstances which may assist in determining what intention is properly to be attributed in Parliament when creating the offence.

More recently, it was found in *R v M and Another (2009)* that the offence of bringing a prohibited article into prison contrary to s.40C(1)(a) of the Prison Act 1952 was not a strict liability offence. (The Offender Management Act 2007 and The Serious Crime Act 2015 have introduced Amendments to the Prison Act 1952)

*****

Chapter 3

Homicide-Unlawful Killing

The distinction between murder and manslaughter
The most common definition of murder is 'the killing of a human being with malice aforethought'. This basically means that a person intended to kill another; the killing was pre-meditated.

Manslaughter can be either voluntary or involuntary. Voluntary manslaughter arises where the definition of murder seems to have been satisfied but one of three defences can be pleaded. These are diminished responsibility, provocation and the survivor of a suicide pact. Involuntary manslaughter occurs where there is no malice aforethought, no intention but a death occurs because of an involuntary act or an act of gross negligence. We will be discussing manslaughter further on in the book.

Murder and manslaughter share the same *actus reus* which is the unlawful killing of a human being. The *mens rea* for murder and voluntary manslaughter is killing with intent whilst the *mens rea* for involuntary manslaughter will vary and will be explored later.

Murder
As we have seen, murder is a common law offence and not an offence laid down by statute. If convicted of murder the judge will impose a mandatory life sentence.

The definition of murder

The famous judge and former Lord Chief Justice of England, Coke, set out his early definition of murder. This is said to arise where:

A man of sound memory and the age of discretion unlawfully killed within any county of the realm any reasonable creature in rerum natura under the King's peace, with malice aforethought, either expressed by the party or implied by law, so that the party wounded or hurt etc die of the wound or hurt etc within a year and a day after the same.

As with many areas of the law this early definition has changed over the years.

Current definition of murder

The current definition of murder can be said to be 'the unlawful killing of an human being under the Queens peace with malice aforethought'. The killing must be the result of an unlawful act and certain acts are not considered criminal. For example, killings by execution, killings by the armed forces or police in the line of duty and certain deaths (in very limited circumstances) accelerated by the medical profession are not considered to be unlawful. The victim (obviously) must be human. Murder or manslaughter is not relevant in law if the victim is an animal. Newborn babies which are barely recognisable as a human being are covered by the law although obviously the debate over this is strong and ongoing. The courts must decide when life begins. Normally, a foetus must have been expelled from the mother's womb and have an independent existence. One case which emphasised this was *Rance v Mid-Downs Health Authority 1991* where it was stated that a baby is capable of being born alive if it can breathe through its own lungs. An attack on an unborn child, either by the mother herself or by another would usually only result in a charge of abortion or child destruction. However, if damage is occasioned to the unborn child and it is subsequently born then a charge of manslaughter can be brought (Attorney General's reference (no 3 of 1994)).

Under the Queen's peace
Most victims of murder would come within this category.

Malice aforethought
This is an old expression and misleading. The actual words 'malice aforethought' merely means that the accused intended to cause death or grievous bodily harm. Although there existed some doubt as to whether the intention to cause grievous bodily harm was sufficient intention to murder, the case of Cunningham 1982 made clear that the intention to cause serious harm was enough.

If a person intends to take the life of another, he is said to have express malice. If the intention is to cause serious bodily harm, then this is implied malice

Chain of causation
The death of another must have been caused by the unlawful death of the defendant. The defendant does not have to have been directly responsible for the actual final act that resulted in the death of another person but will still be liable for the

homicide because he was responsible for the chain of events that led up to it.

Courts look at several issues when deciding the guilt or otherwise of the defendant:
- Did the conduct of the accused cause the resulting harm (what was the factual cause of death?)
- Was the defendant also liable in law?

When deciding on the factual cause of death the courts will use the 'but for' test, i.e., but for the act of the defendant, the death would not have occurred.

After initially satisfying the test of factual causation, the courts still need to be shown that the defendant's act was a significant cause of the death and that no act in between, or intervening act, had broken the chain of causation. The defendant can escape liability if he or she can demonstrate that some other act had caused the death.

Several cases highlight the difficulty of establishing intervening acts. In *Pagett 1983*, as we have seen, the accused was being chased by police and had then taken his pregnant girlfriend captive after injuring her mother and stepfather. He used his girlfriend as a human shield when trying to escape and in the process aimed a shot at the police who in turn fired back killing the girlfriend. The defendant was found guilty of her manslaughter and tried to get this charge overturned by stating that the jury had been misdirected in saying that he was the cause of the death instead of the police officer. The Court of Appeal found that there was no misdirection. Patently the chain of events were set in motion by the accused.

In *Williams 1992*, the prosecution had claimed that the deceased person had jumped from a car because he was in fear of being robbed. To support this, it was alleged that his wallet had flown into the air as he jumped. The victim had 'hitched' a lift from the defendants. He had jumped out five miles on and had been killed. The defendants were originally held to be liable for the death but appealed. The Court of Appeal stated that the conduct of the victim had to be proportionate to the threat of harm and quashed the conviction.

Voluntary manslaughter

This crime is similar to murder in that an unlawful homicide has taken place with the intention to kill, or malice aforethought. However, special circumstances exist which allow for the less serious charge of involuntary manslaughter.

As stated, there are three defences to murder which can result in voluntary manslaughter: diminished responsibility, provocation and survival of a suicide pact.

Diminished responsibility

The law on diminished responsibility can be found in s.2 of the Homicide Act 1957 as substituted by s.52 of the Coroners and Justice Act 2009 which came into force on the 4th of October 2010. Section 2 of the 1957 Homicide Act, (as substituted by the Coroners and Justice Act 2009 s.52) states that a person may be found guilty of voluntary manslaughter rather than murder if he was suffering from an abnormality of mind caused by an inside source that substantially affected his responsibility for his actions. Section 2 of the act puts the burden of proof on the defendant. He will have to prove his abnormality of mind on a balance of probabilities and in general must be the one to raise the defence. If the plea of voluntary manslaughter is to be used in an appeal, then strong evidence will need to be shown for this to succeed.

'Abnormality of mind' is defined as a state of mind a reasonable man would find abnormal. Inside source is seen as an abnormality which must be caused by 'arrested or retarded development of mind or any inherent causes or induced by disease or injury'. The abnormality of mind must be demonstrated to be greater than that experienced by an ordinary person. There must be medical evidence in support of the abnormality.

Provocation

This defence was available if the loss of control which led to the act was caused by provocation of another(s). However, provocation has been abolished with the passing of the Coroners and Justice Act 2009, replaced with loss of self- control, outlined below. In relation to the old defence of provocation, whilst it existed S3 of the Homicide Act 1957 states:

'Where, on a charge of murder, there is evidence on which the jury can find that the person charged was provoked (whether by things done or things said or both together) to lose his self control, the question whether the provocation was enough to make a reasonable man do as he did shall be left to be determined by the jury'.

Evidence of provocation

The judge had to decide whether there is enough evidence to be put before the jury. Provocation could arise from either things done or said. The words or actions do not need to have come from the deceased nor need they be directed at the defendant. In *Pearson 1992,* the victim (father) had persecuted and ill-treated the accused person's brother. The Court of Appeal decided that this could be used as a defence after he killed his father with a sledgehammer.

If the accused is the one who has started the trouble, this will be regarded as 'self induced' provocation. A case which illustrates this is Johnson 1989. The accused started an argument in a night club, during which he made threats to the victim and his girlfriend. A fight started and the victim was fatally stabbed. The accused alleged he was provoked by the fear of being glassed by the victim but the judge did not put this matter before the jury.

The Court of Appeal allowed the defendants appeal, despite the fact that he was the one who had started the trouble.

Loss of self-control
In addition to being provoked, the defendant must show that the provocation was strong enough to make him lose his self-control. The standard definition of provocation arose in the case of *R. V Duffy 1949*. In this case, an abused wife killed her husband in bed after a quarrel. The definition in this case allows the defence to be used where the provoking event has caused:

A sudden and temporary loss of self-control rendering the accused so subject to passion as to make him or her, for the moment, not a master of his mind.

There does not need to be a complete loss of control to the extent that the accused does not know what he is doing.

Reasonable man (normal person) acting in a similar way
Although this may seem a simple proposition, it is in fact quite a complex area. Under the Coroners and Justice Act 2009, the term 'reasonable man' has been replaced with the term 'normal man'.

The new test is whether a person of the defendant's sex and age, with a normal degree of tolerance and self-restraint might have reacted in the same or a similar way.

Who or what exactly, is or was reasonable man? The House of Lords, in *R. V Camplin 1978* stated that the reasonable man is said to be a normal man with normal attributes. In this case, a 15-year-old boy had been drinking and went with an older man to the latter's house where the boy was forcibly subjected to a homosexual assault. When he expressed shame at what had happened the older man allegedly taunted him. The boy attacked him and killed him with a pan. He was convicted of murder after a direction from the judge about a reasonable man.

The House of Lords decided that, while certain of the boy's characteristics should not be taken into account, such as his drunkenness and excitability, other characteristics such as age, could be. The question for the jury therefore was whether a reasonable youth with similar characteristics would have acted in the same way. The appeal against murder was upheld.

Following numerous cases and deliberations, particularly *Smith and Morgan 2000*, a reasonable man was seen to be a reasonable person sharing similar characteristics to the accused. Basically, age, physical characteristics and mental characteristics could be taken into account when measuring the effects of provocation.

In the case of Smith and Morgan 2000, the defendant and the victim had been drinking, indeed were both alcoholics and long-standing drinking partners. During an argument over an alleged theft of Smith's tools, Smith became furious over the others ongoing denials. He stabbed his friend to death with a kitchen knife. At his trial he put forward the defences of diminished responsibility and provocation. He claimed to have a depressive illness that affected his actions.

The trial judge directed the jury that the characteristics of mental impairment could only be brought forward when deciding on the gravity of the provocation, they were not relevant to the reasonable man's loss of self control. The accused was found guilty of murder and, on appeal, the Court of Appeal overturned the verdict and substituted a verdict of manslaughter. The House of Lords agreed that the trial judge had erred by telling the jury that the effect of the defendant's depression on his powers of self-control was not material. Now, as we have seen, the reasonable man has been replaced with the normal man. The new test is whether a person of the defendant's sex and age, with a normal degree of tolerance and self-restraint might have reacted in the same or a similar way.

The survivor of a suicide pact

Suicide was a crime (not in Scotland) until the Suicide Act of 1961 was passed. In addition, before the Suicide Act, if another person was involved in the suicide and survived then he or she would be charged with the murder of the person that did not survive. Suicide is no longer a crime and those that aid and abet suicide are treated more leniently than they were.

Under s4 (1) of the 1957 Homicide Act, if two or more people enter into a suicide pact and one or more survives, that survivor is charged with manslaughter and not murder. The burden of proving a suicide pact is on the accused. A suicide pact, under the 1957 Act is defined as: *an agreement between two or more persons which has as its objects the death of all parties to it.*

Infanticide

This is set out in the Infanticide Act 1938. It is an alternative charge to the charge of murder. It is only available to a woman who has killed her child, provided the child is under the age of 12 months. The woman must provide evidence that she did the killing while the balance of her mind was disturbed because she had not fully recovered from the effect of giving birth or because of breastfeeding the child. The prosecution must disprove this.

Abortion

Under s.58 Offences Against the Person Act 1861 it is an offence to try to procure a miscarriage. The offence can be committed by the woman herself or by another by unlawfully administering any poison or other noxious thing or unlawfully using an instrument or any other means. It is not necessary to show that a miscarriage has actually been caused. By s1 (1) of the Abortion Act 1967, there is no offence if the pregnancy is terminated by a registered medical practitioner where two doctors are of the opinion that:

- the pregnancy has not exceeded the 24th week and that the continuance of the pregnancy involves greater risk of

injury to health of the woman or any existing children of her family than if the pregnancy was terminated; or
- at any time during the pregnancy if the termination is necessary to prevent grave permanent injury to the physical or mental health of the pregnant woman; or
- at any time during the pregnancy if the continuance of the pregnancy would involve greater risk to the life of the pregnant woman than if the pregnancy was terminated; or
- there is a substantial risk that if the child were born it would suffer from a serious physical or mental handicap.

Northern Ireland

Abortion was only decriminalised in Northern Ireland in October 2019 and laws were updated in 2020. Terminations are now lawful unconditionally up to 11 weeks and six days, after this, they are only lawful if there are severe or fatal complications with the foetus. There has been much debate about the commissioning of services in Northern Ireland and to date, full commissioning has not taken place.

Involuntary manslaughter

With both murder and voluntary manslaughter, an intention to kill or cause grievous bodily harm has to be proven. This is not the case with involuntary manslaughter. With involuntary manslaughter, it is enough that the defendant has committed an unlawful and dangerous act and death has resulted, or that someone has died through gross negligence on the part of the accused. There are two types of involuntary manslaughter:

Constructive manslaughter and manslaughter by gross negligence.

Constructive (or unlawful act) manslaughter
Constructive manslaughter is also known as 'unlawful act manslaughter'. This is because the defendant has caused the death of another by an unlawful and dangerous act. There is a clear distinction between this form of manslaughter and gross negligence manslaughter as outlined in the case of *R. V Larkin 1943* by Humphreys J:

If a person is engaged in doing a lawful act, and in the course of doing that lawful act behaves so negligently as to cause the death of some other person, then it is for the jury to say, upon consideration of the whole of the facts of the case, whether the negligence proved against the accused person amounts to manslaughter, and it is the duty of the presiding judge to tell them that it will not amount to manslaughter unless the negligence is of a very high degree… That is where the act is lawful. Where the act which a person is engaged in is unlawful, then if at the same time it is a dangerous act, that is an act which is likely to injure another person, and quite inadvertently he causes the death of that other person by that act, then he is guilty of manslaughter.

Three elements therefore have to be established before a person is liable for constructive manslaughter:
- An unlawful act must have been committed.
- The act must have caused death.
- The unlawful act must have been dangerous.

Unlawful act

When a person is charged with constructive manslaughter this is often in the context of assaulting another person or persons. It is not a viable defence to argue that the defendant did not intend to injure the other person.

One case illustrating this is Larkin 1943, as described above where the accused had discovered his mistress with another man and had taken a razor to the scene. Although he alleged that he intended to only frighten the man he in fact stated that his drunken mistress had fallen onto the razor and cut her throat. Notwithstanding this claim, the conviction for unlawful manslaughter was upheld because an assault had been committed which cause the death of the woman.

For any liability to be established the prosecution has the task of establishing that an unlawful act took place. Two cases illustrate where this was not proved. In *Lamb 1967*, the accused person and his friend were playing with a revolver. The gun had two bullets in it none of which were opposite the barrel. The defendant believed the gun was safe and pulled the trigger with the unfortunate result that the gun fired a live round and killed the other. The Court of Appeal quashed the conviction as it believed that an unlawful act had not been committed.

In the other case *R. V Arioboke 1988*, the victim was fearful of violence from another man, with whom he had had ongoing bad relations. The accused had been peering into a train carriage looking for the victim, the victim had panicked and ran across railway lines trying to escape and had been electrocuted. Arioboke was convicted of manslaughter but the Court of Appeal quashed the conviction on the grounds that there had been no actual assault.

In addition to the unlawful act, death must have arisen as a result of it. It does not have to be the sole cause of it but must have significantly contributed to it. There must, however, have been no other intervening act to contribute to it. Although the act was originally seen as being directed against the victim in the case of *R. V Mitchell 1983*, it was determined that an act intended for another person could, under the doctrine of transferred malice, be classed as being directed against the victim. In this case, the accused had tried to push ahead in the queue at a post office and was punched in the mouth by another man. A second punch or push caused the victim of the attack to fall against a woman who broke her leg. Following complications she died and the accused was convicted of manslaughter but appealed. The Court of Appeal had to decide whether the person at whom the act is directed must also be the person who dies. Staughton J stated:

"We can see no reason of policy for holding that an act calculated to harm A cannot be manslaughter if it in fact kills B. The criminality of the doer of the act is precisely the same whether it is A or B who dies".

Another case, *R. V Goodfellow 1986* took this further and decided that the accused could still be liable whether or not the act was directed against a person or not. In this case, the accused was being harassed in his council house and wanted to move. He knew the chances of moving were very slim and set fire to his flat to help facilitate the move. His fire was intended to seem as though the house had been petrol bombed hoping that this would lead to re-housing. However, such was the blaze that Goodfellow's wife, son and son's girlfriend all died in the fire. The Court of Appeal upheld the conviction for manslaughter even though the unlawful act of arson was not specifically directed at the people who died.

Act must also be dangerous

For constructive manslaughter to arise, the act has to also be dangerous. Whether it is dangerous is an objective decision, it must be an act that a reasonable man would regard as dangerous.

The case of *R. V Church 1996* where the defendant panicked after hitting a woman who had mocked his love making abilities, illustrates this. The defendant believed the woman was dead and threw her in the river where she was drowned. The Court of Appeal upheld the conviction for manslaughter stating:

An unlawful act causing the death of another cannot, simply because it is an unlawful act, render a manslaughter verdict inevitable. For such a verdict inexorably to follow, the unlawful act must be such as all sober and reasonable people would inevitably recognize must subject the other person to, at least, the risk of some harm resulting therefrom, albeit it not serious harm.

In a relatively recent case, *R v JM and SM (2012),* V, a nightclub bouncer, and JM and SM were involved in a violent affray outside of the nightclub where V was employed. JM was the instigator of the affray and both JM and SM were involved in it. Although it was not established that JM and SM had directed any violence towards V it was accepted that V was involve din trying to break up the ensuing fight. After re-entering the nightclub immediately after the incident V collapsed and subsequently died of a ruptured renal artery aneurism. The cause of V's death was a rise in blood pressure as a result of the incident. The judge stopped the trial and ruled that the prosecution would have to prove that V died of the type of harm that a sober and reasonable person would inevitably have realised the affray risked causing and that, taking the evidence at it's highest the prosecution had failed to do this.

The prosecution ruled against the judge's ruling and the Court of Appeal held that it was not a requirement of the *Church* test that a reasonable and sober person foresee the "type" of harm suffered by V, it being sufficient that the unlawful act exposed D to a risk of some, albeit not serious harm. In the present case, the affray clearly exposed V to the risk of some harm given the level of violence being used. The fact that the cause of death was not from the type of harm that may have been foreseen was not relevant to the question of dangerousness.

Manslaughter by gross negligence

Manslaughter by gross negligence is caused by an act of negligence that has caused the death of another. One case illustrating this is *R. V Adamako 1995*. In this case Doctor Adamako's actions of negligence caused his patients death. Lord Mackay decided that liability for this type of manslaughter will arise where the jury decides that: *Having regard to the risk of death involved, the conduct of the defendant was so bad in all the circumstances as to amount in their judgement to a criminal act or omission.* In Adomako, it was decided by the House of

Lords that the gross negligence test is the correct one to use in all cases where a duty of care has been broken.

However, the principles of civil and criminal law do not always sit well together. The case of *R. V Wacker 2003* demonstrated this. This case involved the bodies of 58 illegal immigrants and two survivors which were found in a lorry at Dover. The deaths arose because the container was sealed from the outside preventing oxygen from entering. The defendant was convicted of 58 counts of manslaughter by gross negligence and appealed. He argued that because the illegal immigrants had shared the same purpose as him, i.e. to gain illegal entry to the UK, he did not owe them a duty of care. The Court of Appeal rejected this argument. It decided that the public policy issues relating to civil law were different to criminal law and even where there was an underlying illegal purpose this did not prevent criminal liability arising. The conviction in this case was upheld.

Killing a child or vulnerable adult
The Domestic Violence, Crime and Victims Act 2004, (as amended) s.5 created the offence of causing or allowing the death of, or serious physical harm to, a child (someone under 16) Or a vulnerable adult (someone over 16 "whose ability to protect himself from violence, abuse or neglect, is significantly impaired through physical or mental disability or illness, through old age or otherwise"). The maximum punishment is 14 years in prison.

Corporate manslaughter
In July 2007, the Corporate Manslaughter and Corporate Homicide Act was passed which created a specific offence under

section 1 (1) of 'corporate manslaughter' under which an 'organisation' is guilty 'if the way its activities are managed or organised (a) causes a person's death, and (b) amounts to a gross breach of a relevant duty of care owed by the organisation to the deceased'. Section 1(2) identifies various 'organisations' including corporations, partnerships, police forces and many government departments. Section 1(3) states that liability under s. 1(1) will follow only if the way in which the organisations activities are managed or organised by its 'senior management' is a 'substantial element in the breach'.

One main case here is that of *Cotswold Geotechnical Holdings Ltd 2012*. The company was concerned in soil investigation. In order to obtain a soil sample in the course of the investigation a pit was dug to a depth of 3.5 metres. The pit was entirely unsupported and collapsed upon the employee of the company who had entered it to obtain the relevant sample. The employee died of traumatic asphyxia. The company was convicted of corporate manslaughter on the basis that it was in gross breach of its duty of care to the deceased by not enforcing a strict prohibition on entering pits of such depth without ensuring that the proper shoring was in place. A fine of £385,000 was upheld on appeal even though it resulted in the company entering administration.

Another case of Corporate Manslaughter, was that of *Wood Treatment Ltd*. Wood Treatment and its representatives were charged following a joint investigation carried out by Cheshire Constabulary and the Health and Safety Executive (HSE). This followed an explosion and fire at Bosley Mill in Stoke on Trent which happened on July 17th, 2015, and killed a number of people. The manslaughter case was dropped in 2021 but the company was fined £75,000.

Causing death by driving

Prompted by the reluctance of juries to convict motorists of manslaughter, Parliament enacted an additional offence in the Road Traffic Act 1988 s.1 of causing death by dangerous driving, with a maximum sentence of 14 years.

1n 1991, s.3A was inserted into the Road traffic Act 1988 creating the offence of causing death by careless driving whilst unfit through drink or drugs or above the drink/drive alcohol limit. The Road Safety Act 2006 inserted a new s.28 into the Road Traffic Act 1988 creating a further offence of causing death by careless or inconsiderate driving (maximum sentence 5 years). The 2006 Act also inserted into s.3ZB of the 1988 Act an offence of causing death by driving whilst unlicensed, disqualified, or uninsured. In *R. v Hughes (2013)* the Supreme Court determined that "causing death" in the context of this offence entailed more than mere factual causation and required some element of fault on behalf of D.

*****

Chapter 4

Non-Fatal Offences Against the Person

Assault

The essence of assault is that the victim is put in fear. An assault, or common assault, arises when the person accused of assault intentionally or recklessly causes the victim to apprehend immediate and unlawful violence. In the case of Ireland 1998, the House of Lords confirmed the above definition. If the offence is assault however, this concerns the inflicting of actual harm.

Assault and battery are separate offences and are contained within s.39 of the Criminal Justice Act 1988, which repealed s47 of the Offences against the Person Act 1861. The Criminal Justice Act 1988 states that common assault and battery are to be treated as summary offences with a maximum sentence of six months.

Common assault and battery can only be tried in the magistrates' court, unless the attack is racially motivated, in which cases the offences can be tried in the magistrates' court or Crown Court by virtue of the Crime and Disorder Act 1998 (CDA 1998).

Assaults on Emergency Workers

The Assaults on Emergency Workers (Offences) Act 2018 (AEWOA) 2018) provides for increased sentencing powers for offences of common assault and battery committed against an emergency worker acting in the exercise of functions as such a worker from 13 November 2018.

Actus reus of assault

The actus reus of assault occurs when the accused causes the victim to apprehend immediate and unlawful violence. No force need be applied. Any conduct which causes the victim to believe that he or she is to be assaulted can amount to an assault.

In the case *of R. v Wilson 1955*, Lord Goddard stated that words alone can constitute an assault. In the case of Ireland 1988 the House of Lords also decided that silence can amount to an assault. In this case, the accused terrorised women with silent phone calls.

The threat of assault

The victim must believe that immediate violence is about to be inflicted on him, although the courts will interpret this liberally. Provide the victim believes that he might be subjected to immediate violence, the fear need not be completely rational. In *Smith v Chief Superintendent of Woking Police Station 1983*, it was stated 'When one is in a state of terror, one is very often unable to analyse precisely what one is frightened of as likely to happen next'. In this case, the victim was frightened by the accused who was staring at her through the windows of her home. The defence in this case argued that the action could not have constituted assault because all windows and doors were locked. The Appeal Court held that it was enough that the woman felt herself to be in danger of having violence inflicted on her.

In another case, *Constanza (1997)* D stalked his victim over a period of two years. He followed her home from work, made silent telephone calls, sent over 800 letters, visited her against her express wishes and wrote offensive words on her front door. He sent her two letters which she interpreted as threats. She believed that he might do something to her at anytime. She was diagnosed with clinical depression.

He appealed against his conviction for assault occasioning actual bodily harm, arguing that there had been no assault (a) because the victim can have no fear of immediate violence unless the victim can see the alleged assailant, and (b) an assault cannot be committed by words alone.

Dismissing the appeal, the Court of Appeal held that both these arguments were wrong. The principles established in Ireland above were upheld, that silence can amount to an assault.

Mens rea of assault

This is satisfied when the defendant intends to cause the victim to apprehend immediate physical violence or does this recklessly. The mens rea of assault was confirmed in the House of Lords in *Savage (1991)* In Savage D threw a glass of beer at her victim. In the process D lost grip of the glass which and cut her victims wrist. D was convicted of inflicting serious bodily harm. On appeal this was reduced to assault occasioning bodily harm. there was a further appeal to the House of Lords, arguing that she had not foreseen that her actions would cause bodily harm. The Lords dismissed her appeal.

Battery

This offence arises when the defendant intentionally or recklessly applies unlawful physical force to another person. The difference between assault and battery is that an assault is committed where the victim believes that he is likely to be subjected to harm and a battery takes place only where force is applied. The definition and all elements of the offence of battery are set out in case law. The punishment for battery (maximum 6 months imprisonment) is set out in statute under s.39 Criminal Justice Act 1988.

Definition of battery

In *R v Ireland* [1997] 3 WLR 534 Lord Steyn defined battery as:

"unlawful application of force by the defendant upon the victim"

In addition, The Offences Against The Person Act 1861, Section 47, makes it an offence, punishable by 5 years imprisonment, to commit an assault occasioning actual bodily harm. The word "assault" here is used to mean either an assault or a battery.

The law starts with the assumption that an individual has the right to be protected from molestation. In the case of *Collins v Wilcock 1984,* Goff L J stated' the fundamental principle, plain and incontestable, is that every person's body is inviolate'.

The above also applies to the police when apprehending a person. They are not allowed to grab or touch a person unless making an arrest. The touching of clothing can also constitute an assault. In the case of Thomas 1985 the rubbing of a girl's skirt was held to amount to battery.

Not all touching is unlawful.
In Collins v Wilcock, it was noted:

Most of the physical contacts of ordinary life are not actionable because they are implicitly consented by all who move in society and so expose themselves to risk of bodily contact.

One case which illustrates this is *Donnelly v Jackman 1970*, where the court held that the officer in question did not commit a battery when he tapped on the other's shoulder to attract attention. Obviously, it is a question of degree.

Indirect battery
Battery need not be directly inflicted on the victim. *Scott v Shepherd 1773* illustrated this. In this civil case, the court held that the defendant had committed a battery when he threw an illegal squib into a marketplace. Two people picked it up and threw it away and it injured one of them.

In *Martin 1881*, the defendant placed an iron bar across an exit in a theatre, turned off the lights and shouted 'fire'. In the panic that followed several people were injured. The defendant's conviction for grievous bodily harm was upheld.

The actus reus and mens rea of battery
The *actus reus* consists of the application of unlawful physical force on another. The *mens rea* is satisfied when the defendant intends to carry out such an act or is reckless about whether force will be applied.

Consent as a defence

If the alleged victim has given consent to the alleged crime committed against him then no offence will have been committed.

However, the consent must be one that the law recognises as a valid one. These circumstances are limited. In *R. v Coney 1882*, the courts held that a bare-fist prize fight was illegal, despite the agreement of the parties. In another case, Leach 1969, it was held that the defendants were guilty of assault, even though the victim had consented to being crucified on Hampstead Heat.

Consent may be available 'for properly conducted games and sports, lawful chastisement or correction, reasonable surgical interference, dangerous exhibitions etc'. Practical joking and consent to minor harm in sexual activities are also limited defences.

Lord Templeman stated that in cases where no actual bodily harm had been caused, the consent of the person affected stops him from complaining. He also added that Parliament, under the Sexual Offences Act 1967 had permitted homosexual activities in private between consenting adults. However, he refused to accept the contention of the accused that their sexual appetites could only be satisfied by inflicting serious harm on another:

"*sado-masochism is not only concerned with sex. It is also concerned with violence. The evidence discloses that the practices of the appellants were unpredictably dangerous and degrading to mind and body and were developed with increasing barbarity and taught to persons whose consents were dubious or worthless*".

The message is clear in this summing up. He added ' I am not prepared to invent a defence of consent for sado-masochistic encounters which breed and glorify cruelty and which result in offences under sections 47 and 20 of the Act of 1861.

In summary, the current position on consent in cases of assault and battery is as follows:
- It can be a defence, in certain and appropriate cases of ordinary assault and battery.
- It will not usually be a defence in cases of actual and grievous bodily harm.
- It will not be available to those who transmit sexual diseases even if the other has consented to intercourse.
- It could be available in the case of sexually transmitted diseases if the defendant has clearly accepted the risk.

Actual Bodily Harm

Section 47 of the Offences Against Persons Act 1861 covers actual bodily harm, although the legislation has been modified by future Acts such as the 1956 Sexual Offences Act and in Northern Ireland by the 2003 Sexual Offences Act. The act does not define what constitutes actual bodily harm although case law has developed this. The offence is a triable either way offence and there is a maximum sentence of five-years if the case is tried in the Crown Court. If the magistrates agree and the defendant chooses a Magistrates Court trial then the case can be dealt with summarily.

Actual bodily harm is a form of aggravated assault. Before it is decided that the victim has suffered harm then it is necessary to establish that he has been subject to either assault or battery

Defining actual bodily harm

In the case of *Miller 1954,* the term 'actual bodily harm' was said to include 'any hurt or injury calculated to interfere with the health and comfort of the victim'. In the case of *R. v Chan-Fook 1994*, the Court of Appeal stated that 'actual bodily harm'

"are three words in the English language which require no elaboration and in the ordinary course should not receive any. The word 'harm' is a synonym for 'injury'. The word 'actual' indicates that the injury should not be so trivial as to be wholly insignificant...The body of the victim includes all parts of his body, including his organs, nervous system and brain. Bodily injury therefore may include injury to any of those parts of his body responsible for his mental and other faculties".

Malicious wounding or grievous bodily harm

Section 20 of the OAPA 1861 states that: 'whosoever shall unlawfully and maliciously wound or inflict any grievous bodily harm upon any person, either with or without any weapon or instrument shall be guilty of an offence'. The maximum punishment for this offence is five years.

Malicious wounding or grievous bodily harm is further defined under s18 of the OAPA 1861, which has been amended by the Criminal Law Act 1967. This section states:
'Whosoever shall unlawfully and maliciously by any means whatsoever wound or cause any grievous bodily harm to another person...with intent to do some grievous bodily harm...or with the intent to resist or prevent the lawful apprehension or detainer of any person, shall be guilty of an offence'.

The maximum sentence for a s.18 offence is life imprisonment. This distinguishes it from a s.20 offence. In addition, the harm cannot have been inflicted recklessly, there must have been an intention to cause harm. The s18 offence is committed when the judges feel that the accused caused grievous bodily harm which had a wider meaning than that described under s.20.

Harassment and stalking

In the mid 1990's a number of stalking cases came to court and the offenders were charged under the Offences Against the Person Act 1861. However, there was a redefinition of the law, the result being the Protection from Harassment Act 1997 which has been amended by subsequent legislation. The Protection of Freedoms Act 2012 inserted the offence of stalking in relation to this section and is defined to include things like monitoring a person online, contacting a person, loitering in a public or private place, interfering with property or spying/watching a person.

Section 3A was inserted into the Protection From Harassment Act 1997 by section 125(5) of the Serious Organised Crime and Police Act 2005. This section provides similar injunction provisions to those in section 3, but in this case applying to the offence created by section 1(1A). However, in addition to it allowing the person who is the victim or who may be the victim of the conduct in question to seek an injunction, it also gives a similar right to someone whose behaviour the harassment is intended to influence.

*

Protection from Stalking Act 2019

The majority of stalking offences take place in a domestic abuse setting, but there remains a number of stalking offences that are perpetrated by strangers.

It is this 'stranger stalking' that the Stalking Protection Act 2019 is designed to tackle, and as part of the government's ongoing plan to address violence against women and girls. It came into force on 15 March 2019.

The Act's main purpose is to introduce stalking protection orders (SPOs), which can be applied for by the police to prevent the stalker from continuing their abuse of the victim. The SPO can be put in place before any criminal prosecution takes place, allowing for the victims to be protected from an earlier stage.

The SPO can both order the stalker to refrain from taking certain action (such as visiting the victim's place of work or making contact with them) and require them to take specific action (such as attend a mental health assessment).

The Act also makes it a criminal offence to breach the SPO without a reasonable excuse, which carries a prison sentence of up to five years.

Harassment

It is an offence to pursue a course of conduct which amounts to harassment of another and which the accused knows, or ought to know, amounts to harassment (ss.1 and 2) PFHA 1997. As few as two incidents can amount to harassment but only if there is a connection between them *(Lou v DPP (2000))*. the incidents comprising harassment could occur within a space as brief as five minutes: *R. v Kelly (2003)*.

A course of conduct could be classed as a single offence of harassment even if directed towards more than one person., providing these persons were a close-knit definable group living in the same house: *DPP v Dunn (2000)*.

Putting the victim in fear of violence

A person whose course of conduct causes another to fear, on at least two occasions, that violence will be used against him commits an offence under s.4 if he knows or ought to know that his course of conduct will cause the other to fear violence against him on each of those two occasions. The maximum sentence is five years.

Racially or religiously aggravated harassment

The Racial and Religious Hatred Act 2006 came into force on 1 October 2007. It created new offences of stirring up religious hatred, which are significantly different from the race hate offences contained within Part III of the Public Order Act 1986.

Northern Ireland

The Protection from Harassment (Northern Ireland) Order 1997 (SI 1997/1180) (NI 9) was made under paragraph 1 of Schedule 1 to the Northern Ireland Act 1974 (as modified by section 13 of this Act) only for purposes corresponding to those of sections 1 to 7 and 12 of this Act.

Scotland

In Scotland the Act works differently. Civil remedies include damages, interdict and non-harassment orders backed by powers of arrest. Any person who is in breach of a non-harassment order made under section 8 is guilty of an offence and liable, on conviction on indictment, to imprisonment for a term not exceeding five years, or to a fine, or to both, and, on summary conviction, to imprisonment for a period not exceeding six months, or to a fine not exceeding the statutory maximum, or to both. A breach of a non-harassment order is not otherwise punishable.

Some Scots lawyers are of the view that there was no need for this Act to extend to Scotland because the law of Scotland already dealt satisfactorily with harassment and contained no relevant lacuna corresponding to any which existed in English law.

*****

Chapter 5

Sexual offences

See also chapter 8-Cyber Crime.

The Sexual Offences Act 2003 reformed the law on sexual offences by consolidation of pre-existing laws. It abolished some former criminal offences (repealing most of the Sexual Offences Acts 1956 and 1967 and the Indecency with Children Act 1960) and created a new law on rape and sexual assault as well as a host of other new offences including offences committed against vulnerable people.

It should be noted that the Serious Crimes Act 2015 has modified the 2003 Act by:

- replaceing anachronisticreferences to child prostitution and child pornography in the Sexual Offences Act 2003
- introducing a new offence of sexual communication with a child
- creating a new offence making it illegal to possess paedophile manuals

The Act applies to England and Wales only, which we will be discussing. The corresponding legislation in Scotland is the Sexual Offences (Scotland) Act 2009 and in Northern Ireland the Sexual Offences (Northern Ireland) Order 2008.

In this chapter, we will focus on four key areas: rape, assault by penetration, sexual assault and child sexual offences.

Rape

Under the Sexual Offences Act 2003, s.1(1) a person (A) commits an offence if-

a) he intentionally penetrates the vagina, anus or mouth of another person (B) with his penis,
b) B does not consent to the penetration, and
c) A does not reasonably believe that B consents.

The offence can be broken down into four elements:

- Penetration with the defendant's penis of the complainant's vagina, anus or mouth;
- The complainant did not consent;
- The penetration was intentional;
- The defendant did not reasonably believe that complainant consented.

The first two elements contain the *actus reus* of the offence, the second two the *mens rea*.

Penetration

The first aspect of the *actus reus* concerns the physical act. SOA 2003, s. 79(2) defines penetration as 'continuing act from penetration from entry to withdrawal'. This definition means that an initially lawful act becomes rape if consent is revoked during intercourse. This mirrors the position under the old law, except that the offence is widened to include penetration of or by surgically constructed body parts (in particular through gender reassignment surgery) and oral penetration (anal penetration was formerly covered within the Criminal Justice and Public Order Act 1994).

Mens Rea
Intention to Penetrate
For these purposes, all that is required is that the act of penetration is a deliberate or voluntary one *(R v Heard [2008]*

No Reasonable Belief in Consent
This is not an entirely objective test, in that section 1(2) provides that regard should be had to all of the circumstances.

Particular personality traits or a particular mental disorder might be relevant to whether a defendant can be considered to have a reasonable belief in consent *(R v Braham [2013]*.

Self-induced intoxication cannot give rise to a reasonable belief in consent *(R v Grewal [2010]* Section 1(2) does not require a defendant to take positive steps in an attempt to ascertain whether a complainant is, in fact, consenting.

Consent
Section 74 of the SOA 2003 provides that:
For the purposes of this Part, a person consents if he agrees by choice, and has the freedom and capacity to make that choice.

A complainant may or may not consent without any extrinsic demonstration of their frame of mind.

The issue of consent is further complicated by the fact that it can cover a range of reactions ranging from reluctant agreement to an express desire for the penetration to occur *(R v Watson [2015).*

Until relatively recently a woman could not refuse to have sexual intercourse with her husband. This position was changed in *R v R [1992] 1 AC 599*

There are two roles for consent in the offence of rape. One is-did the victim consent to the act in question and the other is did the defendant have a reasonable belief that the victim was consenting? Lack of consent is part of the *actus reus* of rape. The 2003 Act provides greater guidance than the old laws by creating three different approaches to consent. The main definition of consent is found in s.74 of the SOA 'A person consents if he agreed by choice and has the freedom and capacity to make that choice'. However, section 75 and 76 cover other approaches to defining whether or not consent was given. Section 75 applies to the following:

a) there has been violence towards the victim or the victim fears violence
b) there has been violence towards a third party or the victim fears that violence will be used against a third party
c) the victim has been unlawfully detained
d) the victim was asleep or otherwise unconscious
e) the victims physical disability precluded communication about consent
f) a substance had been administered to the victim which has, or could, overpower or stupefy him.

Section 76 applies to situations where there has been:
a) deception as to the nature or quality of the act
b) impersonation of another

The relationship between the presumptions under s.76 and the wider definition of consent in s.74 was considered by the Court of Appeal in the case of *R v. Jheeta 2007*. The facts of the case were that the defendant (D) and victim (V) met at a college and started a consensual sexual relationship. V began to receive anonymous threatening text messages. D (who had, in fact, sent the messages) reported the matter to the police on V's behalf. She subsequently received texts sent from various police officers assigned to the case (which turned out to be from D) over a period of 3-4 years. During this time V attempted to end the relationship with D This coincided with texts from the police telling her to have intercourse with V and that she would be arrested and fined if she did not. D was eventually charged with rape.

Belief in consent
Under the previous law, a defendant could avoid liability for rape if he had an honestly held belief in consent, even if that was unreasonable. The current law reversed this position introducing the requirement that the defendant' belief in consent must be reasonable.

One particular problematic area is to be determined when the victim is extremely intoxicated. The courts have found that if the victim has lost capacity to choose to consent then consent was not given. However, if the victim was capable of choosing whether to have intercourse then consent was given. This was demonstrated in the case *R v Bree (2007)*.

Assault by penetration
Section 2 SOA provides:

A person(A) commits an offence if:
- he intentionally penetrates the vagina or anus of
- another person (B) with a part of his body or anything else,
- the penetration is sexual,
- B does not consent to the penetration, and
- A does not reasonably believe that B consents. The mens rea of this offence is identical to that discussed above in relation to rape. The actus reus differs in two respects. The first difference is that penetration can be with any part of the defendant's body or anything else.

The second actus reus element requires the penetration to be sexual.

Section 78 SOA provides:
For the purpose of this Part (except section 71) penetration, touching or any other activity is sexual if a reasonable person would consider that –
- whatever its circumstances or any person's purpose in relation to it, it is because of its nature sexual, or
- because of its nature it may be sexual and because of its circumstances of the purpose of any person in relation to it (or both) it is sexual.

The requirements of section 78(a) are reasonably clear, in that where an act is clearly sexual in nature. Indeed, even if the defendant's intentions are entirely non-sexual, if the act itself is clearly sexual, the act will satisfy section 78(a).
    The application of section 78(b) is slightly more complex. Where the question as to whether the act is sexual is ambiguous,

the jury must consider firstly whether, in its view, the nature of the act may make it sexual and, if it does, whether in the particular circumstances of it, it was in fact sexual *(R v H (2005)*.

Sexual in nature

the only unexplored element concerns the requirement that the penetration must be sexual in nature. 'Sexual' in relation to this is defined in s.78 SOA 2003. Penetration, touching or other activity is sexual if a reasonable person would consider that-

a) whatever its circumstances or any person's purpose in relation to it, it is because of its nature sexual, or

b) because of its nature it may be sexual and because of its circumstances or the purpose of any person in relation to it (or both) it is sexual.

Sexual assault

Section 3 provides:

A person (A) commits an offence if –

- he intentionally touches another person (B),
- the touching is sexual,
- B does not consent to the touching, and
- A does not reasonably believe that B consents

The only element of this offence which requires consideration is touching and a victim does not necessarily need to be aware that they are being touched *(R v Bounekhla [2006)* Nor does the victim's body need to be touched *(R v H [2005]*.

Causing a Person to Engage in Sexual Activity Without Consent

Section 4 provides:

A Person (A) commits and offence if –
- he intentionally causes another person (B) to engage in an activity,
- the activity is sexual,
    - B does not consent to engaging in the activity, and
    - A does not reasonably believe that B consents

This section also has the effect of making a defendant liable if the victim is forced by the defendant to engage in sexual activity with somebody other than the defendant.

Upskirting

Upskirting" is a colloquial term referring to the action of placing equipment such as a camera or mobile phone beneath a person's clothing to take a voyeuristic photograph without their permission. It is not only confined to victims wearing skirts or dresses and equally applies when men or women are wearing kilts, cassocks shorts or trousers. It is often performed in crowded public places, for example on public transport or at music festivals, which can make it difficult to notice offenders.

The Voyeurism (Offences) Act 2019 received Royal Assent on 12 February 2019 and was implemented 12 April 2019. The new offences apply to England and Wales and they will not be retrospective. These offences are triable either way and carry a maximum 2 year prison sentence.

Prior of the creation of the new offences contained in the Voyeurism (Offences) Act 2019 (the "2019 Act"), no specific offence of upskirting existed. Depending upon the particular circumstances, certain behaviour could be prosecuted under existing law such as the common law offence of Outraging Public Decency, or the existing Voyeurism offences under section 67 of the Sexual Offences Act 2003.

However, this legislation doesn't cover all instances and as such some acts of upskirting could avoid prosecution. By creating a specific upskirting offence the legislation is strengthened and enables courts to ensure the most serious sexual offenders are made the subject of notification requirements.

Child victims
The law makes a distinction between children under the age of 13 and children aged 1-16. Sections 5,6,and 7 of the Sexual Offences act 2003 replicate ss.1,2, and 3 where the victim is a child under 13.

Section 5 covers the rape of a child under 13
Section 6 covers the assault of a child under 13 by penetration
Section 7 covers the sexual assault of a child under 13
The differences between the under 13 offences and those in ss 1-3 are that:
- The child cannot give consent. Any consent given is not legally recognised
- There can be no reasonable belief in consent
- The offence is one of strict liability in relation to age

This means that the relevant offence is complete if intercourse, penetration or sexual touching occurs in relation to a person under the age of 13, irrespective of whether they consented or even instigated the activity-however old they look.

In *R v G (2009)* the defendant, a 15-year old boy, had sexual intercourse with a 12-year old girl who had told him that she was 15 years of age. The complainant subsequently told friends that she had not consented to having sexual intercourse. The defendant was charged with rape of a child under 13. The complainant accepted that she had told the defendant that she was 15. The House of Lords held, in relation to the defendant's appeal against conviction, that proof of the intentional penile penetration of a child under 13 was all that was required for a conviction under section 5. Appeal dismissed.

Sexual activity with a child
The 2003 SOA also introduced the offence of sexual activity with a child. S.9 holds that a person aged 18 or over (A) commits an offence if-

a) he intentionally touches another person (B)
b) the touching is sexual, and
c) either-
(i) B is under 16 and A does not reasonably believe that B is 16 or over, or
(ii) B is under 13.

This offence makes a distinction between children under 13 and children over 13 but under 16. There is a defence where the complainant is under 16, but the defendant reasonably believes that they are 16 or over.

****

Chapter 6

Property Offences

There are two main types of offences against property, namely dishonesty offences and offences involving damage. The key dishonesty offences are theft, handling stolen goods, burglary, robbery and blackmail which are all covered by the Theft Act 1968. The main offences concerning damage are criminal damage, aggravated criminal damage and arson. These are contained within The Criminal Damages Act 1971. On 15 January 2007 the Fraud Act 2006 came into force, redefining most of the offences of deception.

Theft and other related offences
As stated above, the legislation covering theft and other related offences is the Theft Act 1968. Theft is a triable either-way offence and the maximum sentence is seven years.

Sections 1-7 of the Theft Act 1968 covers the law of theft with section 1 defining theft. This definition is that a person is guilty of theft if he 'dishonestly appropriates property belonging to another with the intention of permanently depriving the other of it'. Section 3 of the Theft Act covers the meaning of 'appropriates'. This states:
...any assumption by a person of the rights of an owner amounts to be an appropriation, and this includes, where he has come by the property (innocently or not) without stealing it, any later

assumption of a right to it by keeping or dealing with it as owner. A person therefore appropriates property when he assumes the rights of the true owner. One case illustrating this is *Pitham and Hehl 1977*, where the Court of Appeal decided that a man who invited the two defendants into his friend's house whilst he was in prison and then sold them some of his furniture, had been assuming the rights of the owner. Not all the rights of the owner need to be appropriated. One case that illustrates this is *Anderton and Burnside 1984*. In this case, the shopper had removed the price label from a joint of pork and replaced it with a lower price label from another item. He was arrested and appealed on the basis that he had not appropriated property belonging to another, because he had not assumed the rights of the real owner. The appeal was dismissed after the House of Lords decided that they had assumed at least one of the rights of the real owner.

The law on appropriation can be summarised as follows:
- an appropriation will have taken place when just one of the rights of the owner is assumed;
- an appropriation can occur even though the owner apparently consents to the appropriation (unknowingly);
- an appropriation may still take place where the defendant appears to have acquired legal ownership of the property;
- an appropriation will not, however, take place where the act is not a physical one and is considered too remote.

This last point was illustrated in the case of *Briggs 2003*, where the defendant had handled the purchase of a house called Welwynd Lodge, supposedly for her elderly relatives. She enclosed a letter of authority signed by them, instructing the conveyancers in the sale of the couple's existing property, to send £49,950 of the sale proceeds to the solicitors acting in the sale of Welwynd Lodge and to send the remainder to the relative's bank account. Welwynd Lodge was subsequently registered in the names of the defendant and her father.

The allegation by the prosecution was that the consent of the elderly couple was induced by fraud as they believed that the property was being purchased on their behalf. The defendant was convicted on one count of theft, two counts of forgery, two counts of dishonestly obtaining social security benefits and one count of obtaining property by deception. Briggs was given leave to appeal on the charge of theft only. Although the prosecution had claimed that the defendant had appropriated the credit balance of £49,950 when the conveyancers had transferred the proceeds of the sale to the solicitors involved in selling, the defence argued that a payment transferred in this fashion could not amount to an appropriation within the meaning of s3 of the Theft Act. The Court of Appeal agreed, surprisingly, deciding that the word 'appropriation' required a physical act, not a remote act.

Section 4 (1) of the Theft Act 1968 defines the meaning of 'property' including:
'money and all other property, real and personal, including things in action and other intangible property'.

Section 4(2) qualifies the meaning by stating that a person cannot steal land, or things forming part of the land, except in specific circumstances, such as the unauthorised disposal of land by a trustee or personal representative, where a person not in possession of the land severs something from it or where a tenant removes something from the land which should have remained attached to the land.

'Things in action'
Things in action are known in civil law as 'choses in action'. They consist of intangible property such as copyrights and patents, shares, debts and insurance policies.

Section 4(3) deals with wildflowers, plants and animals. Section 4(3) states that no offence is committed if a person picks wild mushrooms and flowers, fruit, or foliage as long as it is not for commercial purposes. Section 4(4) states that a person will not commit theft if he captures a wild animal which has not been tamed or reduced to captivity.

Section five of the Theft Act 1968 deals with the definition of 'belonging to another'. This section states that:

Property shall be regarded as belonging to any person having possession or control of it, or having in it any proprietary right or interest...

The property can belong to either the owner of it or those who are currently in possession of it or have some right over it. Section six of the Act defines the meaning of 'permanently depriving the other of property'. This covers situations such as the borrowing of property with the intention of returning it. Section seven lays down maximum punishment terms for offences under the Theft Act.

Robbery
Section 8(1) of the Theft Act 1968 defines robbery as:
A person is guilty of robbery if he steals and immediately before or at the time of doing so and in order to do so, he uses force on

any person or seeks to put them in fear of being then and there subject to force.

Section 8(2) of the Act provides for life imprisonment as a maximum sentence. By definition, robbery is aggravated theft so theft must be established first. Several cases highlight the nature of a robbery. In *R v Robinson 1977*, the defendant ran a clothing club and was owed money by the victim's wife. A fight took place during which £5 fell from the victim's pocket. The defendant took this money and further claimed that he was still owed £2.

The Court of Appeal quashed the conviction for robbery as he had a belief that he was entitled to the money and could not be held to have stolen it.

In another case, *R v Hale 1979*, the defendant and an accomplice, wearing stocking masks, forced their way into the victim's house, put a hand over her mouth to stop her screaming and then tied her up. Before tying her up, the accomplice had stolen a jewellery box from upstairs. The defendant was convicted of robbery. He appealed stating that because the theft had occurred before the victim was tied up the definition of robbery had not been established.

The Court of Appeal rejected this argument stating that 'the act of appropriation does not suddenly cease. It is a continuous act and it is a matter for the jury to decide whether or not the act of appropriation has finished'.

Burglary

Section 9 of the Theft Act 1968 defines the offence of burglary in two parts:

Under s.9 (1)(a) the crime is committed where:

- the defendant enters a building or part of one;
- as a trespasser;
- with the intent to steal, inflict grievous bodily harm, or do unlawful damage to the building or anything inside it.
- Under s9(1)(b) the offence is also committed where:
- a person steals or inflicts grievous bodily harm on another;
- after he has entered as a trespasser;
- or attempts to do either of these things.

Elements of burglary

Entry

The entry must have been effective. This was highlighted by the case of *R v Collins 1973*. The defendant, who was 19 years old, had seen the girl in question when he worked near her house and after drinking a lot had decided to visit the premises. On seeing a light in her bedroom, he fetched a ladder to reach the bedroom. On looking through the window he saw the girl lying on the bed naked and asleep. He walked down the ladder, took off his clothes except for his socks and then climbed the ladder. He alleged that as he was pulling himself into the room the girl awoke. According to him she got up, knelt by the bed, embraced him and appeared to pull him towards it. They then had sexual intercourse.

However, the girl argued that she had awoken at about 3.30am and had seen a vague form with blond hair in the open window. She was unable to say whether the person was outside or inside of the window. She had believed that her boyfriend had come to see her but later, during intercourse she had changed her mind and turned on the light.

Collins was later convicted of burglary. The girl argued that she would not have agreed to the intercourse if she had realised that the man in question was not her boyfriend. The defendant claimed that he would not have entered the room if the girl had not have beckoned him. He was convicted and appealed on the basis that he was not a trespasser.

The Court of Appeal decided that there had to have been an entry into the building. Secondly, the defendant needed to have entered as a trespasser, which was more difficult to decide on. Lastly, he had to have intended, at the time of the entry to commit rape.

They stated:

"Unless the jury were entirely satisfied that the appellant made an effective and substantial entry into the bedroom without the complainant doing or saying anything to cause him to believe that she was consenting to his entering it, he ought not to be convicted of the offence charged. The point is a narrow one, as narrow maybe as the windowsill which is crucial to the case. But this is a criminal charge of gravity and, even though one may suspect that his intention was to commit the offence charged, unless the facts show with clarity that he in fact committed it he ought not to remain convicted".

The fact that there must have been an effective entry has since been disputed, such as in the case of *R v Brown 1985*, where the Court of Appeal upheld a conviction for burglary even though the defendant argued that his entry was ineffective because a major part of his body was still on the highway. He had been caught whilst leaning through a shop window and sorting out goods. Therefore, it is the intent and the individual circumstance as well as arguments concerning effective or ineffective entry to a premises.

Trespasser

The courts have held that a person is a trespasser if he enters a premises of another knowing that 'he is entering in excess of the permission given to him or being reckless to this fact'.

Building

Although there is no definition of a building in the Act, s9(4) states that the word includes an inhabited vehicle and a vessel, even if they are not inhabited at the time of the offence.

In *Stevens and Gourley 1859*, a building was defined as 'a structure of considerable size and intended to be permanent, or at least endure for a considerable time'.

Aggravated burglary

Section 10 of the Theft Act 1968 states that: A person will be guilty of aggravated burglary if he commits any burglary and at the time has with him any firearm or imitation firearm, any weapon of offence or explosive.

Section 10(2) gives a wide definition of firearm to include air pistols and any imitation firearm, i.e., something which has the appearance of a firearm whether discharged or not.

Actus reus

For the aggravated offence the actus reus consists of the destruction of or damage to, property.

Mens rea

In addition to intending or being reckless as to the damage or destruction the defendant must intend to endanger life, or be reckless as to doing so. That requirement is absent if the defendant did not foresee a risk that human life would be endangered.

In *R v Steer (1987)* D fired a rifle at the window of a house. No injuries were caused to those inside. he pleaded guilty to aggravated criminal damage then appealed. The House of Lords held that the intention or recklessness envisaged by s.1(2) of the 1971 Act was directed to the possible danger to life caused by the destruction or damage to property. It was not sufficient that D intended or was reckless as to endangering life by shooting. To be guilty under s.1(2) he had to intend or be reckless as to endangering life by the criminal damage, i.e. by the broken glass).

Criminal Damage

Criminal damage is covered by the Criminal Damage Act 1971. Section 1(1) of the Act covers the basic offence of criminal damage. S1 (1) states:

A person who without lawful excuse destroys or damages any property belonging to another intending to destroy or damage any such property or being reckless as to whether any such property would be destroyed or damaged shall be guilty of an offence.

There are really four main criminal damage offences:
- Simple criminal damage that occurs when the defendant intentionally or recklessly destroys or damages property belonging to another.

- Aggravated criminal damage which occurs if the defendant intentionally or recklessly destroys or damages their own or someone else's property intending or being reckless whether life thereby would be damaged.
- Arson that occurs if the defendant intentionally or recklessly destroys or damages property by fire.
- Aggravated arson that occurs if the defendant intentionally or recklessly destroys or damages property, by fire, intending or being reckless whether life would thereby be endangered.

If the damage or destruction to property is less than £5,000 it will be summarily tried in the Magistrates Court. If it is above £5,000 the offence comes into the category of a triable either way offence for which the maximum punishment is ten years imprisonment.

When defining 'destroys' the courts have decided that rendering something useless will constitute destruction. Damage is defined as not total destruction but where property is made imperfect or inoperative.

One case illustrating this is *Samuels v Stubbs 1972* where a policeman's cap was trampled. The courts decided that the word damage 'is sufficiently wide in its meaning to embrace injury, mischief or harm done to the property'.

Property, under the Criminal Damage Act 1971, is defined as all items of a tangible nature, including money and also animals belonging to another. Although the definition of property is similar to the definition in the Theft Act 1968 there are two distinctions to be made:

- Land cannot be stolen but it can be damaged.
- Intangible property, such as patents and copyrights can be stolen but cannot be damaged.

As we have seen, under the basic defence the property has to belong to another. This is not the case for more serious offences. It is not an offence to damage your own property. However, the property has to clearly be one's own. One case that illustrates this is *R. v Smith 1974*, where the tenant of a ground floor flat damaged floorboards, roofing and other areas of a flat before vacating. He claimed that he had caused the damage whilst in the process of removing some of his own electrical wiring. This had been installed with the landlord's permission. He argued that the property belonged to him and he was not liable for criminal damage. Not surprisingly, the Court of Appeal rejected this argument. Property under s.10(2) of the Act is treated as belonging to another if that other has custody or control of it, a proprietary right in it, a charge over it or a right under trust.

This was the case in Smith where although the landlord had given permission by installing the writing the landlord gained a right or control over the installation.

Defences to Criminal damage

Although all of the usual general defences, described later, are available there is a special defence provided in the act, the defence of lawful excuse.

Under s.5 (2) of the Criminal Damage Act 1971, there are two situations where the defendant can claim this special defence:

- Where he believes that the owner has consented to the damage or would have consented had he known of the facts.
- Where he destroys or damages the property of another in order to protect his own or another's property.
- If defence number two is claimed then two further points must be proved:
- The defendant must believe that the property in question was in need of immediate protection
- The methods adopted to protect the property were reasonable in the particular circumstances.

Section 5(3) goes on to state ' It is immaterial whether a belief is justified or not if honestly held'.

Several cases have highlighted the defence of lawful excuse. In *Jaggard v Dickinson 1981*, the defendant was charged with basic criminal damage after breaking into a house belonging to a stranger while under the influence of alcohol. She acted in the belief, mistaken, that the house belonged to her friend. Her friend, so she claimed, would have consented to the breaking of a window if she was aware of the facts. The magistrates convicted her stating that she could not rely on section 5(2)(a) because she was drunk and this was self-induced. The Divisional Court overturned the conviction stating:

...Parliament has specifically isolated one subjective element, in the shape of honest belief, and has given it separate treatment and its own special gloss in s.5 (3). This being so, there is nothing objectionable in giving it special treatment as regards drunkenness, in accordance with the natural meaning of the words.

In *Chamberlain v Lindon 1998*, the defendant demolished a wall built by a neighbour because he believed that it threatened his right of access. The Divisional Court decided that the defendant had an honest belief that his property was in need of immediate protection, and provided that his belief was honestly held, he was entitled to use the special defence.

Aggravated criminal damage
This offence is committed where a person destroys or damages property, either his own or another's, intending danger to the lives of others. The danger to life must come directly from the damage to the property and not another source. This was illustrated in the case of *R. v Steer 1988* where the defendant had quarrelled with his former business partner and had gone to his bungalow in the early hours with a rifle. He woke the occupants by ringing the bell. They looked out to see who it was and he fired one shot in the direction of the occupants plus two further shots, hitting the window and the front door. The occupants were not injured and it was not suggested that the defendant had fired the gun directly at them. The defendant was charged under s1(1) and s1(2) of the Criminal Damage Act and also with possessing a firearm with intent to endanger life. He appealed against his conviction under s1(2) arguing that the danger to life in this case was from the rifle shots and not damage to property. The House of Lords agreed and his conviction was quashed.

Arson
A person can be charged with arson under s.1 (3) of the Criminal Damage Act, in addition to s.1 (1) and s.2 (2) if there is damage

caused by fire. The maximum sentence for arson is life imprisonment should it be committed in its aggravated form.

Damage to computer programmes

The Computer Misuse Act 1990, s.3 (6) provides that 'For the purposes of the Criminal Damage Act 1971 a modification of the contents of a computer shall not be regarded as damaging any computer or computer storage medium unless its effect on that computer or computer storage medium impairs its physical condition'. Instead, a new offence of 'unauthorised modification of computer material' has been created by s.3 (1) of the Act.

****

Chapter 7

Fraud and Non-Payment

As we saw in the previous chapter, in addition to the Theft Act 1968, dishonesty offences can be found in the Theft Act 1978 and the Fraud Act 2006.

Fraud-Elements of fraud
A person is guilty of fraud if he is in breach of any of the sections listed in the Fraud Act 2006, specifically section 1. Subsection 2 provides for different ways of committing fraud. These are:

a) section 2 (fraud by false representation)
b) section 3 (fraud by failing to disclose information), and
c) section 4 (fraud by abuse of position)

In effect, section 1 of the Fraud act 2006 states that there is a single offence of fraud that can be committed in three different ways:

1. by misrepresenting the truth (false representation)
2. section 3 (fraud by failing to disclose information)
3. section 4 (fraud by abuse of position)

False representation
Actus reus
The actus reus of this form of fraud consists of making a false

representation. It can be a representation of fact or law and includes a representation as to a persons state of mind: s.2(3). Section 2(2) provides that a representation is false if it is untrue or misleading.

Mens rea
There are three mens rea requirements:

(a) the person making the representation must have knowledge that it is, or might be, untrue or misleading;
(b) dishonesty; and
(c) an intention to make a gain or cause a loss (or risk causing a loss) to another person by making a false representation.

There are two elements to false representation that need to be taken into account:
- it must be untrue or misleading.
- it can be express or implied.

Untrue or misleading
A false representation involves creating an impression in the mind of another that something which is false is really true.

Express or implied
An express false representation is one in which the falsity is explicitly communicated to the target of the deception and it tends to involve a positive action. An implied representation tends to be more passive and will typically involve the defendant giving a false impression rather than making an explicit false statement.

Dishonesty

In common with other property offences, there is the requirement that the defendant was dishonest. Dishonesty is established by reference to the two stage *Ghosh* test derived from the court of appeal decision in *R v. Ghosh 1982*.

Question 1 - Objective-is the defendants conduct dishonest according to the ordinary standards of reasonable and honest people?

If yes then the subjective question is asked; did the defendant realise that his conduct would be considered dishonest according to the ordinary standards of reasonable and honest people? If yes then dishonesty has been established. if no on both objective and subjective counts then dishonesty has not been established.

Intention to make gain or cause loss

The Fraud Act 2006 s. 5(2) covers this area and states 'gain' or 'loss'.
a) extend only to gain or loss in money or other property
b) include any such gain or loss whether temporary or permanent
and property means any property whether real or personal (including things in action and tangible property)

s.5(3) 'gain' includes a gain by keeping what one has as well as a gain by getting what one does not have.

Fraud by abuse of position

A person commits fraud under s.4 if he occupies a position in which he is expected to safeguard (or not to act against) the financial interests of another person and dishonestly abuses his position. He will, however, only be liable if he intends to make a gain for himself, or to cause loss to another, or to expose another to a risk of loss, by abusing his position.

Making off without payment

The Theft Act 1978 s. 3 covers this area and states that a person who, knowing that payment on the spot for any goods supplied or service done is required or expected from him, dishonestly makes off without having paid as required or expected and with intent to avoid payment of the amount due shall be guilty of an offence.

****

Chapter 8

Cyber crime

At the end of this chapter there is a summary of the Online Safety Bill, which has now passed all hurdles and set to become an Act in 2023.

Cyber crime is an umbrella term used to describe two closely linked, but distinct ranges of criminal activity. The Government's National Cyber Security Strategy defines these as:
- **Cyber-dependent crimes** - crimes that can be committed only through the use of Information and Communications Technology ('ICT') devices, where the devices are both the tool for committing the crime, and the target of the crime (e.g., developing and propagating malware for financial gain, hacking to steal, damage, distort or destroy data and/or network or activity).
- **Cyber-enabled crimes** - traditional crimes which can be increased in scale or reach by the use of computers, computer networks or other forms of ICT (such as cyber-enabled fraud and data theft).

Cyber-Dependent Crimes
Cyber-dependent crimes fall broadly into two main categories:
- Illicit intrusions into computer networks, such as hacking; and

- the disruption or downgrading of computer functionality and network space, such as malware and Denial of Service (DOS) or Distributed Denial of Service (DDOS) attacks.

Cyber-dependent crimes are committed for many different reasons by individuals, groups and even sovereign states. For example:

- Highly skilled individuals or groups who can code and disseminate software to attack computer networks and systems, either to commit crime or facilitate others to do so;
- Individuals or groups with high skill levels but low criminal intent, for example protest hacktivists;
- Individuals or groups with low skill levels but the ability to use cyber tools developed by others;
- Organised criminal groups;
- Cyber-terrorists who intend to cause maximum disruption and impact;
- Other states and state sponsored groups launching cyber-attacks with the aim of collecting information on or compromising UK government, defence, economic and industrial assets; and
- Insiders or employees with privileged access to computers and networks.

Hacking

Hacking is a form of intrusion targeted at computers, including mobile phones and personal tablet devices. It is the unauthorised use of, or access into, computers or networks by

exploiting identified security vulnerabilities. Hacking can be used to:
- gather personal data or information of use to criminals;
- deface websites; or
- launch DoS or DDoS attacks.

Cyber criminals may use a number of methods to hack into a computer system or network. In many cases, the offender may be motivated by personal profit or financial gain.

Disruption of Computer Functionality

Malware (malicious software) spreads between computers and interferes with computer operations. Malware may be destructive, for example, deleting files or causing system crashes, but may also be used to steal personal data. Prosecutors in such cases need to be aware that some programs have a dual use. They have a legitimate function but can also be used for criminal purposes. Types of malware include:
- **Viruses** are one of the most well known types of malware. They can cause mild computer dysfunction but can also have more severe effects in terms of damaging or deleting hardware, software or file. They are self-replicating programs, which spread within and between computers. They require a host (such as a file) in a computer to act as a carrier, but they cannot infect a computer without human action to run or open the infected file.
- **Worms** are also self-replicating programs, but they can spread autonomously, within and between computers, without requiring a host or any human action. The impact

of worms can therefore be more severe than viruses, causing destruction across whole networks. Worms can also be used to drop Trojans onto the network system.
- **Trojans** are malicious computer programs that present themselves as useful, routine, or interesting in order to persuade a victim to install it. This malware can perform functions, such as stealing data, without the user's knowledge and may trick users by undertaking a routine task while actually undertaking hidden, unauthorised action.
- **Spyware** is software that invades users' privacy by gathering sensitive or personal information from infected systems and monitoring the websites visited. This information may then be transmitted to third parties. Spyware can sometimes be hidden within adware (free and sometimes unwanted software that requires you to watch advertisements in order to use it). One example of spyware is key-logging software which captures and forwards keystrokes made on a computer, enabling collection of sensitive data such as passwords or bank account details.
- **Ransomware** is software that can hold your data hostage, for example, a trojan may copy the contents of the 'My Documents' folder into a password- protected file and delete the original file. It will then send a message demanding payment in exchange for access to the folder.
- Malware may be distributed by **spam** - unsolicited or junk email that is not targeted but typically sent in bulk to millions of recipients around the world.

- A **botnet** is a term for a number of internet-connected computers under the control of a botnet controller. Usually the computers that make up a botnet have been infected with code that enables the botnet controller to undertake illegal activity through multiple devices.
- A **DoS** attack is an attempt to make a machine or network resource unavailable to its intended users, to temporarily or indefinitely interrupt or suspend services of a host connected to the Internet.
- DDoS is where the attack source is more than one, and often thousands of, unique IP addresses. A common method is to flood an internet server with so many requests that they are unable to respond quickly enough. This can overload servers causing them to freeze or crash, making websites and web-based services unavailable to users.

Legislation relating to cyber dependent crimes.
The Computer Misuse Act 1990 ('CMA') is the main UK legislation relating to offences or attacks against computer systems such as hacking or denial of service.

The CMA deliberately does not define what is meant by a 'computer', to allow for technological development. However, in *DPP v McKeown and, DPP v Jones* [1997] 2 Cr App R 155 HL, Lord Hoffman defined computer as 'a device for storing, processing and retrieving information'; this means that a mobile smartphone or personal tablet device could also be defined as a computer in the same way as a traditional 'desk-top' computer or 'PC'.

There is jurisdiction to prosecute all CMA offences if there is "at least one significant link with the domestic jurisdiction" (England and Wales) in the circumstances of the case.

Offences under the CMA:

- Section 1 – causing a computer to perform a function with intent to secure unauthorised access to computer material. This offence involves 'access without right' and is often the precursor to more serious offending. There has to be knowledge on the part of the offender that access is unauthorised; mere recklessness is not sufficient. There also must have been an intention to access a program or data held in a computer. Note the offence is committed irrespective of whether access is obtained.
- Section 2 - unauthorised access with intent to commit or facilitate commission of further offence
- Section 3 - unauthorised acts with intent to impair the operation of a computer. The offence is committed if the person behaves recklessly as to whether the act will impair, prevent access to or hinder the operations of a computer. Section 3 should be considered in cases involving DDoS.
- Section 3ZA - unauthorised acts causing, or creating risk of, serious damage, for example, to human welfare, the environment, economy or national security. This section is aimed at those who seek to attack the critical national infrastructure.
- Section 3A - making, supplying or obtaining articles for use in offences contrary to sections 1,3 or 3ZA. Section 3A deals with those who make or supply malware.

- Under section 3(1) of the Investigatory Powers Act 2016 ('IPA'), which came into force on 27 June 2018, it is an offence to intentionally intercept a communication (in the UK and without lawful authority) in the course of its transmission by means of a public or private telecommunication system or a public postal service. Such offences are triable either way and any prosecution requires the DPP's consent.

A similar offence, now omitted under Schedule 10, paragraph 45 of the IPA, existed under section 1 of the Regulation of Investigatory Powers Act 2000 ('RIPA') and continues to apply to offences committed before 27 June 2018.

Offences under sections 170 to 173 of the Data Protection Act 2018 ('DPA') may be committed alongside cyber-dependent crimes. These include:

- Knowingly or recklessly obtaining or disclosing personal data without the consent;
- Procuring the disclosure of any personal data to another person without consent or after retaining personal data without the consent of that person
- Selling personal data disclosed or retained without consent.
- Further guidance can be found in the legal guidance on the DPA.

Cyber-Enabled Crimes

These are crimes which do not depend on computers or networks but have been transformed in scale or form by the use of the internet and communications technology. They fall into the following categories:

- Economic related cybercrime, including:
    - Fraud
    - Intellectual property crime - piracy, counterfeiting and forgery
- Online marketplaces for illegal items
- Malicious and offensive communications, including:
- Communications sent via social media
- Cyber bullying/trolling
- Virtual mobbing
- Offences that specifically target individuals, including cyber-enabled violence against women and girls ('VAWG'):
    - Disclosing private sexual images without consent
    - Cyber stalking and harassment
    - Coercion and control
- Child sexual offences and indecent images of children, including:
    - Child sexual abuse
    - Online grooming
    - Prohibited and indecent images of children
- Extreme pornography, obscene publications and prohibited images

Economic Related Cybercrime

Economic related cybercrimes include unauthorised access, sabotage or use of computer systems with the intention to cause financial gain to the perpetrator or financial loss to the victim. It may involve computer fraud or forgery, hacking to steal personal or valuable data for commercial gain or the distribution of viruses.

Victims may not report these crimes if, for example, they feel that the issue is trivial or do not actually recognise that what has happened to them is in fact a crime. Additionally, where individuals have had their bank account details accessed or hacked, either the bank or the individual or both may not report the crime if the individual is reimbursed by their bank. Similarly, some businesses may not report for the same reasons, or for fear of reputational damage, or may choose to deal with such issues internally.

Fraud
Cyber-enabled fraud is possibly the most common of all cybercrime offences. The internet allows offenders to hide their identities behind websites and email addresses, providing a forum in which they never have to meet a victim in person to commit the crime. Some offenders may also be part of a wider criminal gang who may also never meet each other, with members based anywhere in the world.

Online fraud can be committed in a number of ways. For example:
- **Electronic financial frauds**, for example, online banking frauds and internet enabled card-not-present (CNP) fraud. Internet-enabled CNP fraud involves transactions conducted remotely, over the internet, where neither cardholder nor card is present. Related to this are e-commerce frauds, which refer more generally to fraudulent financial transactions related to retail sales carried out online. Both businesses and customers may be victims.

- **Fraudulent sales through online auction or retail sites** or through fake websites, which may offer goods or services that are not provided. Alternatively buyers may be led to purchase a counterfeit product (when led to believe it was an original). This may also include other retail misrepresentations, such as online ticketing fraud.
- **Mass-marketing frauds and consumer scams**, including but not limited to:
    - **Phishing** scams are a particular kind of mass-marketing fraud: they refer specifically to the use of fraudulent emails disguised as legitimate emails that ask or fish for personal or corporate information from users, for example, passwords or bank account data Phishing attempts can be sent out en-masse to a range of potential targets;
- **Pharming** occurs where a user is directed to a fake website, sometimes from phishing emails, to input their personal details; and
- **Online romance (or social networking/dating website) frauds**. Individuals may be contacted via social networking or dating sites and persuaded to part with personal information or money following a lengthy online relationship.
- Cyber criminals may seek to obtain personal and financial data for fraudulent purposes. Valuable forms of data may include:
- personal information (names, bank details, and National Insurance numbers);
- company accounts;
- client databases; and

- intellectual property (for example, new company products or innovations).
- Action Fraud is the UK's national reporting centre for fraud and cybercrime and more details about specific types of cyber fraud is available from Action Fraud.

Fraud-Relevant Legislation

Offences under the Fraud Act 2006 are applicable to a wide range of cyber-frauds by focusing on the underlying dishonesty and deception. The nature of the offending will dictate the appropriate charges, and prosecutors may also consider offences under the Theft Act 1968, Theft Act 1978, CMA, Forgery and Counterfeiting Act 1981, and Proceeds of Crime Act 2002 ('POCA').

Note that if an offender accesses data, reads it and then uses the information for his/her own purposes, then this is not an offence contrary to the Theft Act. Confidential information per se does not come within the definition of property in section 4 of the Theft Act 1968 and cannot be stolen (*Oxford v Moss* 68 Cr App R183 DC) 1979. It is likely however that this would constitute an offence under section 1(1) CMA. Also, if it was done with the intent to commit or facilitate the commission of further offences, it would constitute an offence contrary to section 2(1) CMA.

Where there are a number of suspects allegedly involved in online fraud, a statutory conspiracy under section 1 of the Criminal Law Act 1977, or common law conspiracy to defraud may be appropriate.

The acts of setting up a false social networking accounts or aliases could also amount to criminal offences under the Fraud

Act 2006 if there was a financial gain, as under section 8 possession or making or supplying articles for use in frauds includes any program or data held in electronic form.

Intellectual Property Crime (Piracy, Counterfeiting and Forgery)
Intellectual property is defined as a right by an owner, of a copyright, design, patent or trademark. Intellectual property crime can cover a wide range of activities, such as the unauthorised use of another's intellectual property, through the manufacture, use, sale/import of the property without prior permission.

Most intellectual property crime falls under the umbrella of counterfeiting goods, where trademarks are wilfully infringed (see below) and breaches of copyrights, which are usually termed as piracy, and the development of technology to enable such offences to be committed.

Piracy is the unauthorised copying of an original recording for profit. Pirated products will often have different packaging to the genuine product and may often take the form of newly created compilations.

The internet may be used to distribute, share or make available pirated music, films, games or other items in the following ways:
- Use of legitimate file sharing technologies to share copies of music and films e without permission of the intellectual property right holder;
- Posting protected content on a webpage without permission, for example, uploading a copy of a new cinema release;

- Streaming live sports matches, or concerts, out to audiences directly over the internet, without permission; and
- Putting protected content, like a video game, into a cyber- locker, or online storage system, and providing the details on how to access the content on the internet, or a specific group of people.

Counterfeiting is when money or currency is forged but may also relate to goods if they are not manufactured or produced by the designated manufacturer or producer given on the label or flagged by the trademark symbol. The internet may be used as a way of counterfeiting goods, and physical copies of pirated media through:
- offering items, either billed as genuine, or clearly fake, for sale through online shops and auction sites, or on social networking sites;
- Setting up and running sophisticated websites, for example which purport to be genuine retail outlets; and
- Using easily available technology to set up websites offering fake goods, either billed as genuine, or clearly fake.
- Forgery involves making a false object or document with the intention to induce somebody to accept it as genuine and thereby act to his own or another's prejudice. Computers (including computer files), mobile phones, social networking and internet sites can all be used in the creation and transmission of forged or falsified instruments or documents. Moreover, the documents or

instruments created can also be used for further offending.

Intellectual Property-Relevant Legislation

Cyber piracy of music/films/e-books and other items is copyright infringement and is an offence under the Copyright Designs and Patents Act 1988. Counterfeiting goods is a trademark infringement and is an offence under the Trade Marks Act 1994.

Consideration should also be given to the Counterfeiting and Forgery Act 1981, Video Recordings Act 2010, the Registered Designs Act 1949. General statutory offences under the Fraud Act 2006 and money laundering offences under Part 7 of POCA should also be considered. In instances where an individual offers fake identity documents online, the Identity Documents Act 2010 is relevant, where the document is one prescribed under section 7.

Online Safety Bill finished and ready to become law

The Online Safety Bill has, on Tuesday 19th September 2023, passed its final Parliamentary debate and is now ready to become law. It is anticipated that it will receive royal assent very soon.

The bill takes a zero-tolerance approach to protecting children and makes sure social media platforms are held responsible for the content they host. If they do not act rapidly to prevent and remove illegal content and stop children seeing material that is harmful to them, such as bullying, they will face significant fines that could reach billions of pounds. In some cases, their bosses may even face prison.

The bill has undergone considerable parliamentary scrutiny in both the Houses and has come out with stronger protections for all. Social media platforms will be expected to:
- remove illegal content quickly or prevent it from appearing in the first place, including content promoting self-harm.
- prevent children from accessing harmful and age-inappropriate content.
- enforce age limits and age-checking measures.
- ensure the risks and dangers posed to children on the largest social media platforms are more transparent, including by publishing risk assessments.
- provide parents and children with clear and accessible ways to report problems online when they do arise.

In addition to its firm protections for children, the bill empowers adults to take control of what they see online. It provides three layers of protection for internet users which will:
- Make sure illegal content will have to be removed.
- Place a legal responsibility on social media platforms to enforce the promises they make to users when they sign up, through terms and conditions.
- Offer users the option to filter out harmful content, such as bullying, that they do not want to see online.

If social media platforms do not comply with these rules, Ofcom could fine them up to £18 million or 10% of their global annual revenue, whichever is biggest — meaning fines handed down to the biggest platforms could reach billions of pounds.

Also added to the bill are new laws to decisively tackle online fraud and violence against women and girls. Through this legislation, it will be easier to convict someone who shares intimate images without consent and new laws will further criminalise the non-consensual sharing of intimate deepfakes.

The change in laws will make it easier to charge abusers who share intimate images and put more offenders behind bars and better protect the public. Those found guilty of this base offence have a maximum penalty of 6 months in custody. Under the bill, the biggest social media platforms will have to stop users being exposed to dangerous fraudulent adverts by blocking and removing scams, or face Ofcom's huge new fines.

The government has recently strengthened the bill even further, by amending the law to force social media firms to prevent activity that facilitates animal cruelty and torture (such as paying or instructing torture). Even if this activity takes place outside the UK but is seen by users here, companies will be forced to take it down.

Anticipating the bill coming into force, the biggest social media companies have already started to act. Snapchat has started removing the accounts of underage users and TikTok has implemented stronger age verification.

While the bill has been in progress, the government has been working closely with Ofcom to ensure changes will be implemented as quickly as possible when it becomes law.

The regulator will immediately begin work on tackling illegal content and protecting children's safety, with its consultation process launching in the weeks after Royal Assent. It will then take a phased approach to bringing the Online Safety Bill's into force.

Cyber Crime

For further details of cybercrimes covering the below:
- Online Marketplaces for Illegal Items
- Malicious and Offensive Communications
- Offences that specifically target Individuals (including Cyber-Enabled VAWG)
- Child Sexual Offences and Indecent Images of Children
- Extreme Pornography and Obscene Publications

Go to:
www.cps.gov.uk/legal-guidance/cybercrime-prosecution-guidance

****

Ch.9

Animal Welfare

The Law and Animal welfare and control of animals
The primary legislation is the Animal Welfare Act 2006, which applies to England and Wales. For further advice on Scotland and Northern Ireland go to:
www.gov.scot/policies/animal-health-welfare/animal-welfare/
www.nidirect.gov.uk/articles/animal-welfare

The Animal Welfare Act 2006 creates offences where:
- unnecessary suffering is caused (section 4)
- animals are mutilated (a prohibited procedure is carried out upon them) (section 5)
- dogs' tails are docked (section 6)
- poisons are administered (section 7)
- animal fights are caused (section 8)

Each section makes provision for the liability not only of those who do the relevant acts, but those who have responsibility for the animal and permit this to happen. Further offences apply for other culpable acts in respect of animal fights.

The Animal Welfare (Sentencing) Act 2021 increased the maximum sentence for all these offences, making them triable either-way and upon indictment carrying a maximum penalty of five years' imprisonment and/or an unlimited fine.

Under section 9 of the Act, those responsible for animals have a duty to ensure their welfare. A person commits an offence under section 9 if they do not take reasonable steps to meet the needs of an animal, which include: a suitable diet and environment; appropriate housing depending upon the requirements of the animal and to be protected from pain suffering, injury or disease. This does not prohibit the destruction of an animal in an appropriate and humane manner. To prove an offence under section 9, the prosecutor has to prove:

- that the appellant has a responsibility for the animal under section 3 of the Act
- the steps that would have been taken by a reasonably competent and humane person in all the circumstances to meet that animal's needs to the extent required by good practice.
- that the appellant had failed to undertake some or all of those steps.
- In R (on the application of Gray) v Aylesbury Crown Court [2013] EWHC 500 (Admin) the Court held that:
- section 9(1) sets a purely objective standard of care which a person responsible for an animal is required to provide.
- section 9 may be charged as well as section 4. The latter requires proof that unnecessary suffering occurred, the former does not. "There can be no objection to a person being prosecuted for both offences in relation to the same animal."

- the defendant can be convicted on both if the conduct proved in relation to the welfare offence is wider than the conduct which can be proved to have caused actual suffering to the animal.

Criminal Damage Act 1971

Where specific animal welfare offences are not available, prosecutors can consider whether damage to property (a pet belonging to its owner) may be charged. In the case of pets which are stolen, the Theft Act 1968 should be considered.

The Dangerous Dogs Act 1991

The 1991 act was introduced by then Home Secretary Kenneth Baker, and was amended in 1997. The Act applies in England, Wales and Scotland, with The Dangerous Dogs (Northern Ireland) Order 1991 having a similar effect in Northern Ireland. The intention of the Act was the protection of the people. Prior to the Act there were no criminal penalties for injuries or deaths caused by dog attacks.

In summary:
- **Section 1**, *Dogs bred for fighting*, prohibits the ownership of certain types of dogs, unless exempted on the *Index of Exempt Dogs*. It is intended to have a preventative effect.
- **Section 2**, *Keeping dogs under proper control* creates a criminal offence of allowing any dog (of any breed or type) to be dangerously out of control, and legal action may be taken against the dog's owner.
- **Section 3**, *Destruction and disqualification orders*, covers orders for destruction of dogs, and orders for prohibiting offenders from the keeping of dogs for a period.

Britain has a long history of various dog legislation in attempts to protect the public. In the ninth century, dog-owners were fined if their dog bit a person. In 1839, fines were exacted for allowing dogs to run loose in London, and owners were liable if their unmuzzled dog attacked a person or other animal. In 1847, it became a criminal offence to let a dangerous dog run loose. The power to confiscate dogs was introduced in 1871. Prohibition of owning a dog as a penalty was available in 1989. The 1991 Act banned four types of dogs and made it an offence for an owner to allow any dog "to be dangerously out of control". In 1997, the Act was amended, relaxing rules and giving courts more flexibility about euthanasia orders. And in 2006, local authorities were empowered to ban dogs from certain public areas to reduce menace and fouling by dogs.

Under the Act, it is illegal to own certain dogs without an exemption from a court. The Act bans the breeding, sale and exchange of these dogs, even if they are on the Index of Exempted Dogs.

The Act applies to four types of dogs:
- Pit Bull Terrier
- Japanese Tosa
- Dogo Argentino
- Fila Brasileiro

The first two are explicitly mentioned in the Act, and the final two were added by the Secretary of State in 1991.

The Act also covers crossbreeds of the above four types of dogs. Dangerous dogs are classified by "type", not by breed label. This means that whether a dog is prohibited under the Act will depend on a judgement about its physical characteristics, and whether they match the description of a prohibited "type". This assessment of the physical characteristics is made by a Dog Legislation Officer (DLO), a police officer experienced in dog handling and dog legislation, who assists in the investigation of dog-related allegations of crime.

On 15/9/23, The Prime Minister Rishi Sunak announced that American XL Bullies would be added to the Dangerous Dogs Act.

Farm animals

The Welfare of Farmed Animals (England) Regulations 2007 are made under the Animal Welfare Act 2006 and set the minimum welfare standards for all farm animals. Schedule 1 sets out conditions under which all farm animals must be kept, with Schedules 2 to 9 providing additional species specific conditions.

The Mutilations (Permitted Procedures) (England) Regulations 2007 are made under the Animal Welfare Act 2006 and make it an offence to carry out a prohibited procedure on a protected animal. For example, one which involves interference with the sensitive tissues or bone structure of an animal.

The Mutilations Regulations 2007 lists those exemptions to which the prohibitions do not apply if certain conditions are met, such as ear tagging for the purposes of identification or castration for the control of reproduction.

****

Chapter 10

Parties to a Crime

If two or more people commit a crime, they are considered to be joint principals. If one party only helps the other with a crime he or she may be known as a secondary offender or accomplice.

The Criminal Law Act 1967 amended the Accessories and Abettors Act 1861. This states that ... *'Whosoever shall aid, abet, counsel and procure the commission of any indictable offence shall be liable to be tried, indicted and punished as a principal offender'.*

The principal offender
The perpetrator of the crime is the principal offender. This, as we have seen can be more than one person. The test to decide who is the principal offender is to discover whether his act is the most immediate cause of the *actus reus* or whether he is merely aiding that cause to be effected.

Secondary offenders
There are a number of different types of secondary offender. There are those who aid a perpetrator of a crime by giving help, support, or assistance. To abet a perpetrator means to encourage, incite, or instigate. Such encouragement would usually be at or near the scene of the crime. To aid or abet implies some sort of active involvement whereas merely being at the scene of the crime doesn't imply involvement.

One case that illustrates aiding and abetting is that of *Wilcox v Jeffrey 1951*, in which the defendant was the owner of a magazine called Jazz Illustrated. He had attended a concert at which a jazz musician had played in direct contravention of an alien's order that prevented him from performing whilst in the United Kingdom. Although there was no direct evidence that the magazine owner had participated in the concert, he had attended and later wrote about the concert which rendered him liable to prosecution.

A person could also aid and abet in cases where he has some responsibility for controlling the other person. One case that illustrated this was *Tuck v Robson 1970*, where the defendant was a licensee of a public house which the police raided after closing time. Three people were charged with drinking after hours and the publican was charged with aiding and abetting.

To counsel
To counsel parties to a crime is to give them advice and encouragement before the crime is committed. One such case which illustrates this is *Calhaem 1985* where the defendant was infatuated with her solicitor. She wished to remove his girlfriend from his life. She hired a private detective to murder the girlfriend. The detective stated that he had no intention of committing the crime but was going along with it and would state that the attempt was unsuccessful. He alleged that he visited the girlfriend's house with this in mind but when she screamed and panicked, he killed her. Despite this contention, the detective was convicted of murder and Calhaem was found guilty of being a secondary offender. She appealed on the grounds that the judge had not directed the jury that her

counselling of the contract killer had to be a substantial cause of the killing. The Court of Appeal rejected her appeal agreeing with the trial judge that the word 'counsel' merely meant to 'advise, solicit or something of that sort' and decided that there was no implication in this word that there had to be a causal connection between the counselling and the crime.

To procure

To procure is to 'produce by endeavour'. Lord Widgery stated that: You procure a thing by setting out to see that it happens and taking the appropriate steps to produce that happening.

Procuring may also take place when the principal offender has no knowledge of it. However, it is necessary for some sort of connection to exist between the acts of the secondary offender and the crime committed.

A secondary offender can be found guilty of aiding, abetting, counselling, or procuring but only one of these elements needs to be present for him to be found guilty.

Knowledge that a crime is to be committed

In Johnson v Youden and Others 1950, it was stated that before a person can be convicted of aiding and abetting the commission of an offence, he must at least know the essential matters which constitute the offence. In *Bainbridge 1960*, it was decided that the defendant need not know of the precise crime that is to be committed, provided that he possesses not mere suspicion 'but knowledge that a crime of the type in question was intended'.

In the case of Bainbridge, six weeks before the crime took place, Bainbridge used a false name and address to purchase cutting equipment. This was later used by the principal offenders to cut through windows and doors to get at the safe in the bank, which they also cut. Bainbridge was charged as an accessory but tried to claim that he did not know the purpose for which the equipment was being used. Whilst he suspected something illegal he believed that his equipment was going to be used for breaking up stolen goods.

The Court of Appeal held that while it was not enough to show merely that the defendant knew that some sort of illegal activity was going on, it was not necessary to show that he knew the exact time and place of the intended crime. His conviction was upheld.

In addition to the knowledge that the crime was going to be committed the prosecution must also prove that the accomplice had the intention to do the acts that assisted or encouraged the crime. One main case which illustrates this is *National Coal Board v Gamble 1959*. The Coal Board, through the actions of an employee was found guilty of aiding and abetting because the intention to assist the principal offender was apparent. The employee of the Coal Board operated a weighbridge and told a driver that his load was nearly four tons overweight. The driver decided to take the risk of driving the load and was issued a ticket to do so by the employee.

The driver's employers were later found guilty of contravening the Motor Vehicles (Construction and Use) Regulations 1955 and the National Coal Board was also convicted as a secondary offender.

****

Chapter 11

Defences in Criminal Cases

Age of criminal responsibility
The age of criminal responsibility in England and Wales is 10 years old. The rules are different in Scotland. The age of criminal responsibility in Scotland is 8 years old. This means a child aged 8 or older can be arrested or charged with a crime. The age of criminal prosecution in Scotland is 12 years old. This means if a child aged 8 to 11 breaks the law, their case cannot go to a criminal court. Instead, their case may go to a Children's Hearing. The hearing will focus on the child's behaviour and circumstances and not the offence. It is no longer possible for a child under 12 to get a criminal conviction.

Children over 10
Children between 10 and 17 can be arrested and taken to court if they commit a crime. They are treated differently from adults and are dealt with by youth courts, given different sentences and sent to special secure centres for young people, not adult prisons.

Young people aged 18
Young people aged 18 are treated as an adult by the law. If they're sent to prison, they'll be sent to a place that holds 18 to 25-year-olds, not a full adult prison.

Below age of ten

The law has the view that a child under ten years of age does not have the capacity to commit a crime. Rightly or wrongly, agree or disagree, this is the law and it is covered by s50 of the Children and Young Persons Act 1933, as amended. It consolidated all existing child protection legislation for England and Wales into one act. It was preceded by the Children and Young Persons Act 1920 and the Children Act 1908. It is modified by the Children and Young Persons Act 1963, the Children and Young Persons Act 1969 and the Children and Young Persons Act 2008. If the crime is a serious one then the child would be put into care and would not be released back into the community until he or she no longer poses a threat to the wider community.

Between ages of ten and fourteen

The Crime and Disorder Act 1998 outlines the position of this age group of offenders. Children of this age are to be held criminally liable for their actions. Previously, this had not been so but a 1996 case on appeal to the House of Lords concerning a boy of 12, observed by the police on private property holding the handlebars of a motorcycle whilst someone else tampered with it effectively created a new precedent treating those between ten and fourteen as liable.

Children of fourteen and over

A child over 14 years of age is entirely responsible for his or her actions.

*

Insanity

Insanity, or insane automatism can be a defence against a criminal act. However, a balance must be struck between the person's insanity and protection of the public. If an offender faces trial and is considered insane then a plea of not guilty due to insanity will be entered. A range of orders can be imposed on the offender to ensure both his own and the publics safety. Orders arise out of the Criminal Procedures (Insanity and Unfitness to Plead) Act 1991, which amended the Criminal Procedure (Insanity) Act 1964.

These orders are:
- Hospital order without time limit mandatory to murder
- Hospital order with time limit
- Guardianship order
- Supervision and treatment order
- Absolute discharge

Unfitness to plead at trial

If, because of state of mind the defendant is unable to appreciate the significance of the trial then he will be classed as unfit to plead.

Insanity at the time of the crime

In this situation the defendant is considered fit to plead but it is claimed, by either the defence or prosecution, that he was insane at the time of the crime. If the defence of insanity is successful a special verdict is recorded, not guilty by reason of insanity.

Defence of insanity under M'Naughton rules

The rules relating to insanity were laid down after the case of *M'Naughton 1843*. The accused in this case had tried to kill the Prime Minister at the time, Sir Robert Peel. However, he shot and killed the Prime Minister's private secretary, Edward Drummond instead. M'Naughton was found not guilty by reason of insanity. Rules arose from this case. These state that a jury should be informed that a person is sane and responsible for his crimes unless it can be proved that, at the time of the crime:

He was labouring under such a defect of reason, from disease of the mind, as not to know the nature and quality of the act he was doing, or if he did know it, that he did not know he was doing what was wrong.

The burden of proof is on the defendant to prove insanity. A defect of reason caused by a disease of the mind rendering him incapable of knowing what he was doing, must be proved.

Non-Insane Automatism

If an outside factor causes the defendant to act like an automaton, this may be raised as the defence of automatism. Non-insane automatism results in a complete acquittal if proved.

The essence of the defence is that the defendant's actions are completely involuntary. In *Hill v Baxter 1958*, acts committed after a series of blows to the head were seen as examples of automatism. In another case, *Whoolley 1997*, the defendant admitted driving very close to a car and a fit of sneezing caused him to crash into this vehicle. The act of sneezing was seen as involuntary and constituted a defence of automatism. There are limits to the defence and each case is obviously considered on its merit.

Intoxication

If a defendant has voluntarily put himself into a state of intoxication, then this will generally not be seen as a defence. However, whilst voluntary intoxication is not a defence in crimes of basic intent such as assault, manslaughter and rape, it might be allowed as a full or partial defence in other crimes such as:

- Aggravated criminal damage with intention of endangering life.
- Theft.
- GBH or malicious wounding.
- Murder, where there is an unlawful killing with malice aforethought.

All these crimes, except for murder, treated as a special case, require some further intention to be established in addition to the basic offence.

Involuntary intoxication

In the case of involuntary intoxication, where the offender was given drink or drugs without his consent or knowledge, a defence might be raised both in cases of specific intent and basic intent.

In some cases, the courts have considered the side effects of drugs as a defence. In the case of *Hardie 1985*, the defendant had finished with his girlfriend and he became very upset and took Valium to calm his nerves. Although he had been assured that the tablets would calm him, he fell asleep and during this sleep started a fire in his wardrobe at the flat he was vacating. Although he was initially found guilty the Court of Appeal quashed the conviction on the basis of the effects of the drug.

Mistakes about the law

Although mistakes about the law will not usually provide a defence there are limited circumstances where this can be considered. They are as follows:

- Where the mistake prevents the formation of the *mens rea* of the crime
- Where there is justification or excuse for the defendant's actions
- Where a statute provides for this, as in the Theft Act 1968 and the Criminal Damage Act 1971.

Self-defence

While it is accepted that a person may generally defend themselves and their property from attack, the courts and Parliament have always been mindful of minimising the risk of encouraging over-zealous retaliation in such a situation. There is always the danger that the defender might take on the role of the attacker.

Force causing damage to property, injury or even death may be justified if the force was reasonably used in the defence of certain public or private interests. There are three situations where force may be used: Self-defence. This is regulated primarily by the common law, although some of the common law principles have now been codified in s.76 of the Criminal

Justice and Immigration Act 2008 (see below): Prevention of crime. This is covered by s.3 (1) of the Criminal law act 1967, which provides that a 'person may use such force as is reasonable in the circumstances in the prevention of crime, -or in effecting or assisting in the lawful arrest of offenders or suspected offenders or of persons unlawfully at large': Defence of property. This is partially but not exclusively covered by s. 5(2) of the Criminal Damage Act 1971.

Two cases highlight self-defence as a defence of mistake.
Williams (Gladstone) 1987, where the defendant mistakenly believed he was observing a mugging taking place and attacked another man. The real situation was that the so-called mugger had grabbed hold of another person because the latter had robbed a woman. The case on appeal was quashed because it was seen as a genuine mistake. In *Beckford 1988*, a policeman who shot a man who had been terrorising his family was able to use the defence of mistake because he thought the man was armed.

The Criminal Justice and Immigration Act 2008
Section 76 of the 2006 Act codifies some, but not all, of the principles of self-defence. Section 76 (3) states that 'the question whether the degree of force used by the defendant was reasonable in the circumstances is to be decided by reference to the circumstances as the defendant believed them to be. 76 (6) states that 'The degree of force used by the defendant is not to be regarded as having been reasonable in those circumstances as the defendant believed them to be if it was disproportionate in those circumstances.

Necessity

In earlier times this defence was available in specific circumstances such as abortion following rape. However, following the case of *Re A (Children) 2000*, the defence of necessity has been extended. In this case, an operation was seen as necessary in order to save the life of one of conjoined twins and the operation would lead to the death of the other twin. The Court of Appeal had to decide whether the doctors would be killing this twin unlawfully or whether the action could be justified in the eyes of the law. The Court of Appeal decided unanimously that the operation would be lawful. It was decided:

- The act was necessary to avoid inevitable and irreparable harm.
- No more was planned to be done than was necessary for the purpose to be achieved.
- The evil to be inflicted was not disproportionate to the evil to be avoided.

Duress

The defence of duress is available if it is proved that the defendant was forced to commit a criminal act because another is using force or threat against him. In *AG v Whelan 1934*, it was stated that the defence of duress exists where the accused is subjected to 'threats of immediate death or serious personal violence so great as to overbear the ordinary powers of human resistance'.

Duress of circumstances

In limited circumstances, the defence of duress of circumstances can be used. The origins of the defence, which is relatively new, began with the case of *Willer 1986*. The defendant believed that he was going out to meet a fellow radio enthusiast but was directed instead down a narrow alleyway where he and his friends were confronted by a gang of youths. They surrounded his car issuing death threats and tried to drag out the occupants. Willer managed to escape by mounting the pavement and driving through a gap in the road. He then discovered that one of his friends was missing. After he tried to rescue his friend, unsuccessfully, he sought help from the police but, astonishingly, was charged with reckless driving. He was convicted but the conviction was overturned on appeal. The Court of Appeal decided that duress was the necessary defence, as opposed to the defence of necessity.

Marital coercion
This is a very limited defence and only applies to a wife who can prove that she committed an offence other than treason and murder, in the presence of, and under coercion of, her husband.

Public and private defence
A person may use force, as long as it is not unreasonably excessive, in the defence of public and private interests such as:
- To prevent crime or to assist in the lawful arrest of an offender.
- Prevent a breach of the peace.
- Protect property or prevent trespass.
- To protect himself from unlawful violence.
- To protect himself from unlawful detention.

****

Chapter 12

Inchoate Offences

Inchoate offences are incomplete offences. The parties involved might have planned the crime but, for various reasons, the crime does not happen.

Attempts to commit a crime
The above is covered by the Criminal Attempts Act 1981. S1 (1) states that a person will be guilty of attempt if:

With intent to commit an offence to which this section applies, a person does an act which is more than merely preparatory to the commission of the offence. S4 (1) goes on to state 'the attempt is punishable to the same extent as the substantive offence'.

The *actus reus* of attempt
This will exist where the party 'does an act which is more than merely preparatory to the commission of the offence'. The law makes a clear distinction between acts which are undertaken merely to prepare for the crime in question and acts done after this time which will amount to an attempt.

More than merely preparatory
In the case of *R. v Jones 1990*, the defendant was unable to accept that his ex-mistress had formed a relationship with another man. The defendant purchased a gun, jumped in the

intended victim's car, pointed the loaded gun at the man and stated 'you are not going to like this'. The intended victim grabbed the gun and threw it out of the window and escaped. The police arrested the defendant who also had another weapon with him, a knife. He claimed that he only intended to kill himself and no one else. He argued that he had three more acts to do before he could be said to be ready to kill anyone: remove the safety catch on the gun, put his finger on the trigger and pull the trigger.

The Court of Appeal agreed that the act of acquiring the gun, loading it and going to the school where the victim was waiting for his daughter was merely preparatory to the commission of the offence. However, once he got into the car and threatened the victim there was sufficient evidence for the consideration of the jury on the charge of attempted murder.

The *mens rea* of attempt

This consists of an intention to bring about the offence. S1(1) states that a person will be guilty of attempt if 'with intent to commit an offence' he does an act which is more than merely preparatory to its commission. Reckless behaviour is not sufficient to create a liability.

Conspiracy to commit a crime

This offence is covered by the Criminal Law Act 1977, as amended by the Criminal Attempts Act 1981 and the Criminal Justice Act 1987. S1 states that the offence of conspiracy to commit a crime will take place when a party agrees with another or others to pursue a course of conduct which, if carried out, will amount to or involve the commission of an offence, or would do so if something had not happened to make the offence impossible to commit.

The *actus reus* of conspiracy
An agreement with others to pursue a course of conduct which, if carried out, will amount to or involve the commission of an offence.

The *mens rea* of conspiracy
Liability is only incurred if the defendant intends to commit the crime. Intention can be implied from the wording of s1 (1) in which it states that a person must agree with another to pursue a course of conduct.

Incitement
Incitement occurs where a person urges another to commit a crime or tries to influence the mind of another. The courts have decided that incitement can be effected by suggestion, argument, persuasion, or by threats or other pressure.

One case that illustrates incitement is that of *Invicta Plastics Ltd v Clare 1976*, where a conviction was upheld when an advertisement was placed in a motoring magazine drawing attention to a product which could be used to evade speed traps. This amounted to incitement.

The *mens rea* of incitement
The defendant must be shown to have intended to bring about the criminal result and used persuasion or pressure to achieve this. However, it is not necessary for the offence to have been committed.

Encouraging or assisting crime

At common law it was an offence to 'incite' someone to commit any offence. This was committed if the defendant encouraged or persuaded someone else to commit an offence, whether or not that offence took place. However, the general offence of incitement was abolished by s.59 of the Serious Crime Act 2007 and three new offences of encouraging or assisting crime have been created instead. However, various specific incitement offences survive, including:

- Soliciting murder (s.4 Offences Against the Person Act 1861).
- Incitement to commit certain sexual acts outside the United Kingdom contrary to the Sexual Offences (Conspiracy and Incitement) Act 1996.
- Inciting a child under 13 to engage in sexual activity, contrary to s.8 of the Sexual Offences act 2003.

Liability under the Serious Crime Act 2007

Sections 44-46 of the Serious Crime Act 2007 create three new offences of doing an act capable of 'encouraging or assisting' crime. The new offences came into force in October 2008. The new offences relate to an act 'capable of encouraging or assisting the commission of:

- an offence with intent to encourage or assist (s.44)
- an offence believing it will be committed and believing that the act will encourage or assist (s.45)

- one or more offences, believing that one or more of them will be committed and believing that the act will encourage or assist (s.46).

The *actus reus* of ss.44 and 45 is identical: they both require the defendant to 'do an act capable of encouraging or assisting the commission of an offence. The *mens reus* requirements are different, however. Section 44 (1) states that the defendant must encourage or assist commission of the offence, while s. 44(2) adds that the defendant is not to be taken to have the necessary intent ' merely because such encouragement or assistance was a foreseeable consequence of his act'. Section 45 states that the defendant must believe that the offence will be committed and that his act will encourage or assist its commission.

Defences of acting reasonably

Section 50(1) of the Serious Crime Act 2007 provides defences to anyone charged under ss.44-46 where they can prove that they:

- knew certain circumstances existed; or
- reasonably believed circumstances to exist,

provided, in either case, that they can also prove that it was 'reasonable' to act as they did in those circumstances.

Defences for victims

Section 51 provides a defence, in certain circumstances, for victims. If the defendant is accused of intentionally doing an act capable of encouraging or assisting another to commit an offence, but the offence exists for 'the protection of a particular category of persons and the defendant falls within a protected category then the defendant has a defence.

Chapter 13

Criminal cases-Police Powers

Police Organisation

Rather than having one national police force, the UK has 45 police forces (at 2023). These are independently locally run police forces, designed to forge links between the police and local communities. Working alongside police officers are Community Support officers (CSO's) civilians employed by police authorities. Their powers include the ability to:

- issue fixed penalty notices for anti-social behaviour.
- carry out searches and road checks.
- stop and detain school truants.
- deprive an individual of their liberty for up to 30 minutes until a police officer arrives, where the suspect fails to provide his name and address or it is reasonably suspected that the details provided are inaccurate.

The Serious Crime and Police Act 2005 created a national investigation agency, The Serious Organised Crime Agency (SOCA) to tackle the heads of organised crime who undertake illegal enterprises such as drug trafficking, paedophile rings and people smuggling. As from October 7th, 2013, this was replaced by the National Crime Agency.

Over time, there has been a general increase in recorded crime, with violent crime on the increase. The police are obviously in the front line dealing with crime as a whole. The main police powers are contained within the Police and Criminal

Evidence Act (PACE) 1984 with amendments and additions made by the Criminal Justice and Public Order Act 1994 and the Criminal Justice Act 2003, also by the Serious Organised Crime and Police Act 2005 (s110). PACE also provides for the codes of practice giving extra details on the procedures for stop and search, detaining, questioning and identifying suspects. These are issued by the Home Secretary.

Police powers

The police have to exercise their powers sensitively and respect the rights of the individual citizen. At the same time, they must also have sufficient powers to enable them to do their job. The law on police powers is mainly contained within the Police and Criminal Evidence Act 1984 and the associated codes of practice contained within section 66 of the act. There are eight codes, which have been revised along the way, with revisions being to codes C, E F and H in 2017 and 2019.

In addition, there have been revisions to Code A from January 17th, 2023, which expands police powers to stop and search vehicles and persons.

- Code A deals with the powers to stop and search.
- Code B for the powers to search premises and seize property.
- Code C deals with detention, treatment and questioning of subjects.
- Code D deals with the rules for identification procedures.
- Code E deals with the tape-recording of interviews with suspects.
- Code F deals with visual recording of interviews.

- Code G deals with Powers of arrest under section 24 the Police and Criminal Evidence Act 1984 as amended by section 110 of the Serious Organised Crime and Police Act 2005
- Code H deals with requirements for the detention, treatment and questioning of suspects relating to terrorism in police custody by police officers. Includes the requirements to explain a person's rights while detained in connection with terrorism.

PACE has been modified by the Policing and Crime Act 2017, which mean that there is now a presumption that suspects who are released without charge from police detention will not be released on bail, a formality which was written in PACE 1984 Section 3.

Powers to arrest-serious arrestable offences
Some of the rules only apply to serious arrestable offences. These include murder, treason, manslaughter, rape, hijacking, kidnapping, hostage taking, drug trafficking, firearms offences and causing explosions likely to endanger life or property. Other arrestable offences may only be considered to be serious if they endanger the state or public order or cause death of a person.

Powers to stop and search
The powers of police to stop and search people or vehicles are contained in sections 1-7 of PACE. The Psychoactive Substances Act 2016 also introduces new powers to stop and search persons and vehicles where there are reasonable grounds to suspect that the person has committed or is likely to commit an offence

under the Act or that the vehicle contains evidence of an offence. Section 1 gives police the powers to stop and search people and vehicles in a public place. A public place has a wide meaning and extends to private gardens if the police officer in question has good reason to believe that the suspect does not live at that address.

To use this power under PACE the police officer must have reasonable grounds for suspecting that the person is in possession of stolen goods or prohibited articles or goods. These include knives and other weapons which can cause harm or be used in burglary or theft.

Voluntary searches
This is where a person is prepared to submit to a search voluntarily. A voluntary search can only take place where there is power to search anyway. Voluntary searches must be recorded.

Other powers to stop and search
Apart from PACE there are also other Acts of Parliament which give the police the right to stop and search in special circumstances. The Misuse of Drugs Act 1971 allows the police to search for controlled drugs and the Anti-Terrorism, Crime and Security Act 2001 gives powers to stop and search where there is reasonable suspicion of involvement in terrorism.

Section 60 of the Criminal Justice and Public Order Act 1994 gives the police an additional power of the right to stop and search in anticipation of violence.

Other powers to stop and search are contained within the below Acts:

section 47 Firearms Act 1968
section 7 Sporting Events (Control of Alcohol etc.) Act 1985
section 4 Crossbows Act 1987
section 2 Poaching Prevention Act 1862
section 12 Deer Act 1991
section 11 Protection of Badgers Act 1992
section 19 Wildlife and Countryside Act 1981
section 139B Criminal Justice Act 1988

Roadside checks
Section 4 of PACE gives police the right to stop and search vehicles if there is a reasonable suspicion that a person who has committed a serious offence is at large in an area.

The power to search premises
In certain circumstances the police have the power to enter and search premises. PACE sets out most of these powers although there are other Acts which provide for this mentioned later. The police can enter a premises without the occupier's permission if a warrant authorising that search has been obtained from a magistrate. This will normally be issued under section 8 of PACE. The magistrate must be convinced that the police have reasonable grounds for believing that a serious arrestable offence has been committed and that there is material on the premises that will be of substantial value in the investigation of the offence. Search warrants are designed to enable the element of surprise and in the process prevent valuable evidence being removed or destroyed. A warrant must specify the premises to be searched and, as far as possible, the articles or persons to be sought. One entry only, on one occasion is authorised and entry

must be at a reasonable hour unless the police can demonstrate the need to enter at another time. They are also required to identify themselves as police officers and to show the warrant on demand. The courts have, however, held that the police do not have to follow these requirements precisely if the circumstances of the case make it appropriate to do otherwise.

Powers to enter premises without a search warrant

Police officers may enter and search premises if it is to arrest a person named in an arrest warrant, or to arrest someone for an arrestable offence, or to recapture an escaped prisoner. This power is set out in section 17 of PACE. Reason for the entry must be given to anyone in the premises. PACE also gives a police officer the right to enter a premises without a search warrant after an arrest if an officer has grounds to believe that there is evidence on the premises relating to the offence for which the person has just been arrested.

To prevent a breach of the peace

There is a right under common law for police to enter premises if there is a need to deal with or prevent a breach of the peace. This right applies even to private homes as was demonstrated by the case of *McLeod v Commissioner of Police for the Metropolis (1994)* in which the police had entered domestic premises when there was a violent quarrel taking place.

Searching with the consent of the occupier of the premises

The police may enter and search premises without a warrant if the occupier of these premises gives them permission to do so. This consent must be given in writing and can be withdrawn.

Unlawful entry and search

If a premises is entered and searched unlawfully, where the police exceed their powers a claim for damages can be made under the tort of trespass.

Powers of arrest

Section 24 of PACE sets out the general powers of arrest, and some of these powers can be exercised by private citizens as well as the police.

Arrestable offences

An arrestable offence is:
1. Any offence for which the sentence is fixed by law. An example may be murder which has a fixed term of life imprisonment.
2. Any offence for which the maximum sentence that could be given to an adult is five years imprisonment.
3. Any other offence which Parliament has specifically made an arrestable offence.

PACE Section 24 as amended by the Serious Organised Crime and Police Act 2005 -Arrests by police and private citizens.

This section allows the police or a private citizen to arrest without a warrant:
1. Anyone who is in the act of committing an arrestable offence.
2. Anyone whom he has reasonable grounds for suspecting to be committing an arrestable offence.
3. Anyone who has committed an arrestable offence.

4. Where an arrestable offence has been committed, anyone for whom he has reasonable grounds for suspecting to be guilty of it.

The police also have the right to arrest anyone who is about to commit an arrestable offence, anyone whom he has reasonable grounds for suspecting to be about to commit an arrestable offence or where there are reasonable grounds for suspecting that an arrestable offence has been committed.

PACE Section 25

Police have further powers under section 25 to arrest for any offence where the suspects name and address cannot be discovered or that there are reasonable grounds to believe that the name and address given by the suspect are false. Section 25 also provides powers of arrest where there are reasonable grounds for believing that arrest is necessary to prevent that person from:
- Causing physical injury to himself or others
- Suffering physical injury (i.e., suicide)
- Causing loss or damage to property
- Committing an offence against public decency
- Causing an unlawful obstruction of the highways

Section 25 also gives the police powers to arrest if the arrest is believed to be necessary to protect a child or other vulnerable person.

Other rights of arrest

The Criminal Justice and Public Order Act 1994 added an extra power of arrest to PACE. This is in section 46A of PACE and gives the police the right to arrest without a warrant anyone who has been released on police bail and fails to attend a police station at an allotted time. The Criminal Justice and Public Order Act also gives police the right to arrest for a variety of new offences in connection with collective or aggravated trespass.

Arrest for breach of the peace

The police have a right to arrest where there has been or is likely to be a breach of the peace. The conditions for arrest for breach of the peace were laid down in *Bibby v Chief Constable of Essex Police (2000)*. These are:

- There must be sufficiently real and present threat to the peace.
- The threat must come from the person to be arrested.
- The conduct of the person must clearly interfere with the rights of others and its natural consequence must be 'not wholly unreasonable' violence from a third party.
- The conduct of the person to be arrested must be unreasonable.

The right to search an arrested person

Where a person has been arrested the police have a right to search that person for anything which might be used to help an escape or anything that might be evidence relating to an offence.

Powers to detain suspect

Once a person has been arrested and taken to a police station there are rules setting out time limits as to detention. The limits will vary and are longer depending on the severity of the offence. There are also rules, contained in PACE relating to treatment of people in detention. The general rules are that the police may detain a person for 24 hours. After this the police can detain a person for a further 12 hours but only with the permission of a senior officer. After 36 hours those detained for an ordinary arrestable offence must be released or charged. For serious offences those detained can be held for a further period but a magistrate's order must be obtained and the maximum detention cannot exceed 96 hours. There is a right to representation. There is an exception under terrorism offences, which allows for detention of 48 hours and up to another 12 days with the Home Secretary's permission.

Rights of detained people
Detainees must be informed of their rights. These include:
- Someone must/can be informed of the arrest.
- Being told that independent legal advice is freely available. and being allowed to consult with a solicitor.
- Being allowed to consult the code of practice.

Detained persons may be interviewed by the police. All interviews carried out at a police station must be tape recorded. Suspects have the right to a solicitor during questioning. If a solicitor is not asked for or is late questioning can commence. If the person is under 17 or is mentally handicapped there must be an 'appropriate adult' present during questioning.

Section 76 of PACE states that a court shall not allow statements which have been obtained through oppression to be used as evidence.

The right to silence

A defendant has the right to remain silent but inferences can be drawn from the silence and used in court. The wording of a caution given to a suspect states:

'You do not have to say anything. But it may harm your defence if you do not mention when questioned something which you later rely on in court. Anything you do say may be given in evidence'.

Searches, fingerprints and samples

When a person is being held at a police station the police do not have an automatic right to search them. However, a custody officer has a duty to record everything a person has with them and if the custody officer thinks a search is necessary then a non-intimate search can be made. A strip search can only take place if it is necessary to remove an article which a person in detention should not be allowed to keep and there is reasonable suspicion that a person may have concealed an article. There are strict rules governing the nature of a strip search and articles of clothing that can be removed at once and in which places.

The police can take fingerprints and non-intimate body samples without the person's consent. Reasonable force can be used to obtain these if necessary.

There are different rules for intimate samples. These are defined in the Criminal Justice and Public Order Act 1994 as:
    a) a sample of blood, semen or other tissue, fluid, urine, or public hair.
    b) a dental impression.

c) a swab taken from a person's body orifice other than the mouth.

These can only be taken by a registered medical practitioner or nurse. Samples can be retained.

Complaints against the police

People who believe that the police have acted unjustly and exceeded their powers can complain and the type of complaint will determine how it is dealt with. Minor complaints are dealt with informally and more serious complaints will be dealt with at a higher level.

The Independent Police Complaints Commission

This was set up in 2004 to supervise the handling of complaints against the police and associated staff, such as Community Support Officers. It has now been replaced (from January 2018) by the Independent Office for Police Conduct. The IOFPC sets down standards for the police to follow when dealing with complaints. They also monitor the way complaints are dealt with by local police forces. The IOFPC will also investigate serious issues including any accident involving death or serious injury, allegations of corruption, allegations against senior officers, allegations involving racism and allegations of perverting the course of justice.

Any member of the public can complain and complaints can be made directly to the IOFPC or through organisations such as the Citizens Advice Bureau or through the Equality and Human Rights Commission or the Youth Offending Team. It is also possible to complain through a solicitor or an MP. Where the police have committed a crime in the execution of their duties criminal action can be brought against them.

Policing and Crime Act 2017-a summary
The Policing and Crime Act 2017 became law on 31st January 2017. The Act further reforms policing and enables important changes to the governance of fire and rescue services. It is intended that the changes will build capability, improve efficiency, increase public confidence and further enhance local accountability.

The main provisions:
- place a duty on police, fire and ambulance services to work together and enable police and crime commissioners to take on responsibility for fire and rescue services where a local case is made.
- reform the police complaints and disciplinary systems to ensure that the public have confidence in their ability to hold the police to account, and that police officers will uphold the highest standards of integrity.
- further support the independence of HM Inspectorate of Constabulary and ensure that it is able to undertake end-to-end inspections of the police.
- enable chief officers to make the most efficient and effective use of their workforce by giving them the flexibility to confer a wider range of powers on police staff and volunteers (while for the first time specifying a core list of powers that may only be exercised by warranted police officers).
- increase the accountability and transparency of the Police Federation for England and Wales by extending its core

- purpose to cover the public interest and making it subject to the Freedom of Information Act 2000.
- reform pre-charge bail to stop people remaining on bail for lengthy periods without independent judicial scrutiny of its continued necessity.
- stop the detention in police cells of children and young people under 18 who are experiencing a mental health crisis (and restrict the circumstances when adults can be taken to police stations) by reforming police powers under sections 135 and 136 of the Mental Health Act 1983.
- amend the Police and Criminal Evidence Act 1984, including to ensure that 17-year-olds who are detained in police custody are treated as children for all purposes, and to increase the use of video link technology.
- amend the Firearms Acts, including to better protect the public by closing loopholes that can be exploited by criminals and terrorists.
- make it an offence to possess pyrotechnic articles at qualifying musical events.
- reform the late night levy to make it easier for licensing authorities to implement and put cumulative impact policies on a statutory footing.
- better protect children and young people from sexual exploitation by ensuring that relevant offences in the Sexual Offences Act 2003 cover the live streaming of images of child sex abuse.
- increase the maximum sentence from 5 to 10 years' imprisonment for those convicted of the most serious cases of stalking and harassment.

- confer an automatic pardon on deceased individuals convicted of certain consensual gay sexual offences which would not be offences today, and on those persons still living who have had the conviction disregarded under the provisions of the Protection of Freedoms Act 2012.

The Police Crime, Sentencing and Courts Act 2022
Background

In December 2019, the Government was elected with manifesto commitments to protect and empower the police by enshrining "the Police Covenant into law", "passing the Police Protection Bill", introducing new powers to "tackle unauthorised traveller camps" and introducing "a new court order to target known knife carriers, making it easier for officers to stop and search those convicted of knife crime". The manifesto also committed to empower the courts to tackle crime, ensuring a fair justice system by introducing "tougher sentencing for the worst offenders and [ending] automatic halfway release from prison for serious crimes"; and toughening "community sentences, for example by tightening curfews and making those convicted do more hours of community payback".

Out of this came the Police, Crime, Sentencing and Courts Act 2022.

This act ensures that the police have access to support, protection, and recognition they deserve by introducing and enshrining in law a duty to prepare an annual Police Covenant Report with regard to the principle that members or former members of the police workforce should not be disadvantaged as a result of working in policing. It also doubles the maximum penalty for common assault or battery committed against an emergency worker from 12 months to two years' imprisonment, ensuring that emergency workers have sufficient protection from the law to enable them to carry out their duties and the maximum penalty reflects the severity of the offense. The act imposes mandatory life sentences for the unlawful act manslaughter of an emergency worker who is exercising their functions as such a worker, unless there are exceptional circumstances. It also introduces a new test to assess the standard of driving of a police officer, to allow the courts to judge their standard of driving against a competent and careful police constable with the same level of training. Finally, it ensures special constables have access to the same support and representation as regular constables through enabling them to join the Police Federation of England and Wales.

The Public Order Act 2023
The Public Order Act 2023 is an Act of the Parliament of the United Kingdom which gave law enforcement agencies in the United Kingdom greater powers to prevent protest tactics deemed "disruptive" such as those used by climate protestors. It received Royal Assent on 2 May 2023.

This bill followed the Police, Crime, Sentencing and Courts Act 2022, which reintroduced measures previously rejected by the House of Lords. As with the previous Act, this bill also received criticism in regard to declining civil liberties in the country. The Joint Committee on Human Rights "called for key measures in the legislation to be watered down or scrapped because the laws would have a "chilling effect" on people in England and Wales seeking to exercise their legitimate democratic rights.

The Act introduces new offences for locking on (with 51-week sentences), interfering with key national infrastructure, obstructing major transport works, causing serious disruption by tunnelling, greater stop and search powers to prevent disruptive protests (including without suspicion), and "Serious Disruption Prevention Orders" "which can restrict people's freedom by imposing conditions on repeat offenders".

The Act is "explicitly targeted at protesters", such as "the current outbreak of climate protests across Britain". The government specifically named the protests of Extinction Rebellion, Just Stop Oil, and Insulate Britain as reasons it is needed. Measures previously rejected by the House of Lords in consideration of the Police, Crime, Sentencing and Courts Act 2022, including banning individuals from protests, were reintroduced.

In January 2023, Prime Minister Rishi Sunak's government had announced plans to amend the Public Order Bill before it becomes law "to broaden the legal definition of 'serious disruption', give police more flexibility, and provide legal clarity on when the new powers could be used."

****

Chapter 14

Hearing Criminal Cases

As the criminal law is set down by the state, bringing a prosecution for breach of criminal law is seen as the role of the state. The majority of prosecutions are brought by the Crown Prosecution Service which is the agency of the state for criminal prosecutions.

In Scotland the Crown Office and Procurator Fiscal Service (COPFS) is Scotland's prosecution service. They receive reports about crimes from the police and other reporting agencies and then decide what action to take, including whether to prosecute someone. They also investigate deaths that need further explanation and investigate allegations of criminal conduct against police officers. In Northern Ireland the Public Prosecution Service carries out the same role. We will be covering the procedures in England and Wales in this Chapter.

A criminal prosecution can also be brought by an individual or company although this is rare. The following is an outline of the procedure for criminal trials.

Pre-trial hearings
All criminal cases will first go to the magistrate's court and, in most cases, will be referred to a higher court unless the offence is minor or the person(s) plead guilty.

Categories of criminal offences

Criminal offences are divided into three main categories as follows:

1. Summary offences. These are the least serious and are nearly always tried in the Magistrates Court. They include nearly all driving offences, common assault and criminal damage of less than £5,000. The following summary offences can be included on an indictment and tried in the Crown Court :
    - Common assault (Section 39 Criminal Justice Act 1988)
    - Assaulting a prison custody officer (Section 90(1) Criminal Justice Act 1991)
    - Assaulting a secure training centre custody officer (Section 13(1) Criminal Justice and Public Order Act 1994)
    - Assaulting a secure college custody officer (Paragraph 14 or 24 of Schedule 10 to the Criminal Justice and Courts Act 2015)
    - Taking a vehicle without consent (Section 12 Theft Act 1968)
    - Driving while disqualified (Section 103 Road Traffic Act 1988)
    - Low value criminal damage (Section 22 and Schedule 2 of the Magistrates' Courts Act 1980)
    - Triable either way offences. These are a middle range type offence and can include assault causing actual bodily harm. These cases can be tried either in the Magistrates Court or the Crown Court.

- Indictable offences. These are more serious crimes such as rape or murder. All such offences must be tried at the Crown Court, the first hearing being at the Magistrates Court.

Bail

One matter to be decided pre-trial is that of bail, whether the defendant should stay in custody while awaiting trial or whether he or she should be released on bail. Being granted bail means that the person is at liberty until the next stage of the case.

The police may release a suspect on bail while they pursue their enquiries. The suspect must return to the police station at a specified date in the future. The police can also grant bail to a defendant who has been charged with an offence. In this case the person is bailed to appear at a Magistrates Court at a later date. The decision on whether to grant bail or not is made by a custody officer under section 38 of PACE. Bail can be refused if the suspects name and address cannot be ascertained or there is doubt as to the validity of information.

The principles as to when bail should be granted are contained within the Bail Act 1976. This is the key Act, starting with the assumption that an accused person should be granted bail, though this right can be limited for certain cases such as terrorism or repeat serious offences. Section 4 of the Bail Act 1976 gives a general right to bail, but this can be withdrawn if the court believes that there are grounds for believing the defendant, if released, would fail to surrender to custody, commit an offence whilst on bail or interfere with witnesses or obstruct the course of justice. In deciding whether to grant bail the court will consider various factors:

- The nature and seriousness of the offence
- The character of the defendant and community ties
- The record of the defendant
- The strength of evidence against the defendant.

The courts have the powers to impose conditions on the granting of bail. These are like those granted to the police, as outlined below.

Bail and the Policing and Crime Act 2017

It was intended that the Act, which became law on 31st January 2017, should improve decision making and reduce distress and injustice for individuals placed on bail. Accordingly, On Monday 3rd April 2017, The Policing and Crime Act made it a legal requirement for the police to limit the pre-charge bail period to 28 days.

BAIL – The Criminal Procedure (Amendment) Rules 2023

The CPAR Rules 2023 have significantly modified the process of bail and the Police and Crime Act 2017.

As we have seen above, pre-charge bail (also known as police bail) is a process by which a person is released from custody after being arrested pending further investigation – whilst also possibly being subject to certain bail conditions. They are required to return to the police station at a specified date/time whereby they are given an update on their case. At this point, they may be charged, have their bail extended, be Released Under Investigation (RUI), or be released with No Further Action (NFA).

The Government legislated through the Policing and Crime Act 2017 to address concerns that individuals were being kept on pre-charge bail for lengthy periods. The reforms introduced a 'presumption' against pre-charge bail unless it is necessary and proportionate in all circumstances. They also brought about clear statutory timescales and processes for the initial imposition and extension of bail, including the introduction of judicial oversight for the extension of pre-charge bail beyond 3 months.

After these reforms came into force in April 2017, the use of pre-charge bail fell – this was reflected by an increasing number of individuals who were RUI'd. This raised concerns that pre-charge bail was not always being used where it might have been appropriate.

The Criminal Procedure (Amendment) Rules 2023 (CPAR 2023) have now brought about significant changes to the way that pre-charge bail is managed. These reforms have been brought about for a multitude of reasons. A major driving force is to dissuade the use of RUI which has been subject to criticism since its introduction in 2017. This was partly in response to the murder of Kay Richardson, who was killed by her ex-partner while he was RUI and not subjected to bail conditions.

Building on this, another downside to RUI is that many people have been RUI'd for lengthy periods – sometimes for over a year – without knowing anything about the status of their investigation. It can be argued that being RUI leaves people in an unfair 'legal limbo' where they don't quite know where they stand for extended periods of time.

*

The new system
The CPAR 2023 has modified how pre-charge bail works. Sections 47ZA and 47ZB of the Police and Criminal Evidence Act 1984 limit the period for which a person may be subject to pre-charge bail. This period may be extended in specific circumstances by a senior police officer/Court. This was overhauled in 2020 by the Police, Crime, Sentencing and Courts Act 2022 which lengthened the time period for which people can be subject to pre-charge bail. Additionally, pre-charge bail can also be extended by police officers of rank inspector and above for up to 6 months, and extended by officers of rank superintendents or above by up to 9 months:

"Under sections 47ZC and 47ZD of the 1984 Act, in a standard case the applicable bail period may be extended on the authority of a police officer of the rank of inspector or above until the end of 6 months from the bail start date. Under section 47ZDA the applicable bail period may be further extended on the authority of a police officer of the rank of superintendent or above until the end of 9 months from the bail start date."

Building on the above, the CPAR 2023 has now further extended the period to which a person can be kept on pre-charge bail by a Magistrates' Court (and others). They replaced all references to '12 months' in The Criminal Procedure Rules 2020 to '24 months', such that it now states:

"Under section 47ZF of the 1984 Act, on an application made before the date on which the applicable bail period ends by a constable, a member of staff of the FCA of the description

designated by its Chief Executive, an officer of Revenue and Customs, an NCA officer, a member of the SFO or a Crown Prosecutor, a Magistrates' Court may authorize an extension of that period –

- (a) from a previous total of 9 months to a new total of 12 months or, if the investigation is unlikely to be completed or a police charging decision made within a lesser period, a new total of 18 months (following extension under section 47ZDA of the Act);
- (b) from a previous total of 12 months to a new total of 18 months or, if the investigation is unlikely to be completed or a police charging decision made within a lesser period, a new total of **24 months** (following extension under section 47ZDB or 47ZE of the Act)."

For the reasons mentioned above, a major function of the newly introduced CPAR 2023 is that it will promote the use of pre-charge bail as opposed to RUI, due to the fact that pre-charge bail can now be in effect for longer periods, i.e., up to 24 months. It can also be extended purely by the prerogative of inspectors/superintendents and above, as mentioned above. Under previous rules, the police could only release a person on pre-charge bail for up to 3 months – any extension beyond this period required judicial oversight via an application made to the Magistrates' Court.

One concern is that the police now have a greater deal of control over an individual's liberty before they have even been formally charged with a crime. On the other hand, the new rules are expected to have multifaceted benefits. For instance, upon release from custody, people will have much more clarity regarding their case moving forward; pre-charge bail involves firm deadlines so that people know how long they are on bail for and ensures that they are informed about the status of their case. Additionally, the timeframes set on pre-charge bail may encourage the police to work more expeditiously than if the individual was RUI'd (which has no set deadline). Another view is that it would provide additional safety measures to potential complainants through the use of bail conditions.

Bail sureties
The courts or police can require a surety for bail. This is another person who is willing to pay a sum of money if that person doesn't turn up to court. No money is paid until the defendant breaks bail.

If any person granted bail by the police fails to attend the next stage of the case then the police can make an arrest.

Like the courts, the police have powers to impose conditions on bail. These are contained within the Criminal Justice and Public Order Act 1994. These conditions can vary, ranging from surrender of passport to regular reporting at a police station.

Key changes have been introduced in the Policing and Crime Act 2017, as below:
- There is a presumption of release without bail unless the necessity and proportionality criteria are met.
- Where these criteria are met a maximum 28 day period of pre-charge bail can be granted by an Inspector.

- This period can be further extended to a period of three **months** by a Superintendent.
- An applicable bail period (ABP) will be set by the authorising officer and this is the window of time in which a custody officer may set and vary bail.
- The Applicable Bail Period can only be further extended by a Magistrates' Court upon application by the police.
- There are longer time limits for cases designated as 'exceptionally complex' for example SFO investigations.

Bail for CPS Advice

The provisions above do not apply when a suspect is bailed for CPS advice under section 37 (7)(a) of the Police and Criminal Evidence Act 1984. The custody officer will retain the power to grant bail in such circumstances.

Where a suspect is initially bailed for further enquires but then referred to the CPS for a charging decision the ABP Clock will be suspended. The ABP clock will then start again should the CPS request further police work as part of the investigation.

If the police are not prepared to grant bail then they must bring the suspect before a magistrate's court. The magistrates can then make a decision as to whether the suspect should be released on bail.

Restrictions on bail do exist, such as terrorism cases and situations where there have been repeated serious offences.

Section 19 of the Criminal Justice Act 2003 amended the Bail Act 1976 and placed certain restrictions on bail for adult drug offenders who have tested positive for specific Class A drugs where the offender is either charged with possession or possession with intent to supply a Class A drug or the court is satisfied that there are grounds for believing that misuse of a class A drug contributed to the offence or that the offence was motivated wholly or partly by the intended misuse of a drug and the defendant has refused to participate in an assessment or follow up in relation to the dependency on Class A drugs.

The prosecution in a case can appeal against the granting of bail. This is set out in the Bail (Amendment) Act 1993.

The Crown Prosecution Service

The Crown Prosecution Service (CPS) was established by the Prosecution of Offences Act 1985 and began life in 1986. The head of the CPS is the Director of Public Prosecutions who must have been a qualified lawyer for 10 years. The DPP is appointed by the Attorney General. Under the DPP are Chief Crown Prosecutors who each head one of 42 areas. Each area is subdivided into branches, each of which is headed by a Branch Crown prosecutor. Within branches there are lawyers and support staff who are given responsibility for cases. The functions of the CPS involve all aspects of prosecution as outlined below:

- Deciding on what offences should be charged
- Reviewing all cases given to them by the police to see if there is sufficient evidence to proceed and whether it is in the public interest to do so
- Taking responsibility for the case
- Conducting the prosecution of cases in the Magistrates Court
- Conducting cases in the Crown Court

Once a defendant has been charged with an offence then the police role in the matter is over and the case is handed over to the CPS.

Criminal courts
The two courts that hear criminal cases are the Magistrates Court and the Crown Court. If a defendant in either one of these courts pleads guilty to a charge against them the role of the court is to pass sentence. Where the accused pleads not guilty the role of the court is to try the case and establish whether the defendant is guilty or not guilty. The burden of proof is on the prosecution who must prove the case beyond reasonable doubt. The form of trial is adversarial with prosecution and defence presenting their cases and cross-examining witnesses while the role of the judge is to be a referee, overseeing the trial and ensuring that the law is adhered to. The judge does not investigate the case.

The role of the Magistrates Court
There are about 330 Magistrates Courts in England and Wales. Magistrates Courts are local courts and they will be in almost every town whilst big cities will usually have several. Cases are heard by magistrates, who may be either qualified District Judges or unqualified lay justices. There is a legally qualified clerk attached to each court to provide assistance. Magistrates Courts have jurisdiction in a variety of matters. They will:
- Try all summary cases.
- Try any triable either way offences which it has been decided should be dealt with in the Magistrates Court.

- Deal with the first hearings of all indictable offences.
- Deal with other matters connected to criminal offences such as issuing warrants for bail and deciding bail applications.
- Try cases in the Youth Court where the defendant is aged 10-17.

The Magistrates Courts also have some civil jurisdiction including enforcing council tax demands and issuing warrants of entry and investigation to utilities such as gas and electricity, family cases and proceedings concerning the welfare of children under the Children Act 1989.

Summary Trials

Summary trials are the least serious criminal offences. They are further divided into offences on different levels ranging from level one (lowest) to level five (highest). Fines are set in accordance with each level. These fines arise from the Criminal Justice Act 1991 and are increased periodically to account for inflation. The maximum prison sentence that can be given for summary offences is 15 months following the passing of the Criminal Justice Act 2003.

At the start of any summary trial the defendant will be asked whether he or she pleads guilty or not guilty. If a guilty plea is entered the case will be explained to the court and the prosecutor and defence will put their case and the magistrates will decide sentence. If a not guilty plea is entered, the procedure is rather more complicated as the prosecutor has to provide evidence to the court and prove the case. Witnesses are called. At the end the defence can call for the case to be dismissed on lack of evidence if this is the case. The magistrates will then decide on the case, whether guilty or not guilty.

Triable either-way cases- Plea before venue

Under this procedure the defendant is asked whether he pleads guilty. If the plea is guilty then there is no right to ask to go to a Crown Court although the magistrate may still decide to send him there for sentence. If the defendant pleads not guilty then the magistrates must carry out 'mode of trial' proceedings to establish where the case will be tried. Under section 19 of the Magistrates Court Act 1980 they must consider the nature and seriousness of the case and decide a course of action. If the case involves complex cases of law it will usually be referred to the Crown Court.

It will also be referred to the Crown Court if it is of a particularly serious nature and has, for example, involved organised crime or where the amount involved was particularly high, more than twice the potential fine that magistrates can levy.

In cases, rare cases, where the Attorney General, Solicitor General or Director of Public Prosecutions is the prosecutor, magistrates must abide by the wishes of the prosecutor and send the case to the Crown Court if this is what is wanted.

If magistrates accept jurisdiction, the defendant is informed that he has the right to trial by jury, in the Crown Court, but may be tried by magistrates if he so wishes. If the magistrates feel that they have insufficient powers to punish they can refer the matter to the Crown Court for sentencing.

Sending cases to the Crown Court

For indictable offences the case is automatically referred by magistrates to the Crown Court. Section 51 of the Crime and Disorder Act 1988 dictates this. For triable either-way offences, magistrates will hold a plea before venue and, if the plea is not guilty, a mode of trial hearing. The decision to try the case in the Magistrates Court or the Crown Court is taken at this point.

Committal proceedings

Magistrates can commit a defendant charged with a triable either-way offence for sentence in the Crown Court.

Youth courts

Youth offenders aged between 10-17 are dealt with in the Youth court which is a branch of the Magistrates court. Children under the age of 10 cannot be charged with a criminal offence. There are some exceptional cases where the case can be tried in the Crown Court if the charge is one of manslaughter or murder, rape or causing death by dangerous driving. In addition, it is possible to send a person over 14 to the Crown Court if the charge is sufficiently serious.

Appeals from the Magistrates Court

The system of appeal routes from the magistrate's court will depend on whether the appeal is on a point of law or for other reasons.

The two appeal routes are the Crown Court or the Queens Bench Divisional Court. The normal route of appeal is the Crown Court and can only be used by the defence. If the defendant has pleaded guilty then the appeal can only be against sentence. If the plea was not guilty then the appeal can be against conviction or sentence. In both cases the defendant has the automatic right to appeal.

Further appeal to the Supreme Court

From the decision of the Queens Bench Court there is a possibility of a further appeal to the Supreme Court. This can only be made if the Divisional Court certifies that a point of law of general public importance is involved or The Divisional Court or the Supreme Court gives leave to appeal because the point is one which ought to be considered by the Supreme Court.

The Crown Court

The Courts Act 1971 set up the Crown Court to deal with all cases that were not tried at the Magistrates Court. The Crown Court sits in 90 different centres throughout England and Wales.

There are three kinds of centre:

1. First tier-these exist in main centres throughout the country. At each court there is a High court and a Crown Court. The Crown Court is staffed by High Court Judges as well as Circuit Judges and Recorders. The court can deal with all categories of crime triable on indictment.
2. Second tier-this is a Crown Court only, but High Court judges can sit there on a regular basis to hear cases, as well as Circuit Judges and Recorders.
3. Third tier-this is staffed by Circuit judges and Recorders. The most serious cases are not usually tried here.

Preliminary matters in the Crown Court-The indictment

The indictment is a document which formally sets out charges against a defendant.

Disclosure by prosecution and defence

The Criminal Procedure and Investigations Act 1996 places a duty on both sides to make certain points of the case known to each other. The 1996 Act also imposes a duty on the defence in cases which are to be tried on indictment. After the prosecutor's initial disclosure, the defence must give a written statement to the prosecution setting out:

1. the nature of the accused person's defence.
2. the matters on which he takes issue with the prosecution and why he intends to take issue.
3. any point of law which he wishes to take, and the case authority on which he will rely.

Details of alibis and witnesses he intends to call to support the alibi. This information gives the prosecution time to carry out police checks on the witnesses.

A preliminary hearing called a 'plea and directions' hearing is held after a case has been forwarded to a Crown Court, normally within four weeks if the defendant is being held in custody and six weeks if not. The purpose of this hearing is to discover whether the plea is guilty or not guilty. All charges are read out in open court and the defendant will plead one way or the other. This is called the 'arraignment'. If the defendant pleads guilty the judge will sentence the defendant immediately, if possible. Where a defendant pleads not guilty the judge will require the defence and prosecution to identify the key issues of fact and law that are involved in the case. He will then give directions that are necessary for the organisation of the trial.

The trial

A defendant appearing at the Crown Court will usually be represented by a barrister and sometimes a solicitor. Defendants can represent themselves and can, in most cases, cross-examine witnesses although there are some cases where this cannot happen, such as sexual offences. The order of events at a trial will depend on whether the defendant pleads guilty or not guilty. If the plea is not guilty the following will happen:

- The jury is sworn in to try the case.
- The prosecution will make an opening speech outlining the case to the jury.
- The prosecution witnesses give evidence and can be cross examined by the defence-other evidence can be produced.
- At the end of the prosecutions presentation the defence can state that there is no case to go to the jury: if the judge decides that this is so then he will direct the jury to acquit the defendant.
- The defence may make an opening speech provided that they intend calling evidence other than the defendant.
- The defence witnesses give evidence and are cross examined by the prosecution.
- The prosecutor makes a closing speech pointing out the strengths of the case to the jury.

- The defence makes a closing speech pointing out the weaknesses of the case.
- The judge sums up the case to the jury and directs them on any law relevant to the case. The jury retire to consider their verdict.
- The jury returns and gives their verdict
- If the verdict is guilty the judge then sentences the accused, if not guilty the defendant is discharged.

It is normal, once acquitted, that the defendant cannot be re-tried. However, Under the Criminal Justice Act 2003 the double jeopardy rule was removed for serious cases if new and compelling evidence comes to light.

In January 2010, the first trial without jury took place in the Royal Courts of Justice. This will happen rarely in the case of trials where intimidation and jury tampering is feared. Trial without jury, or the powers to hold such a trial are contained within the Criminal Justice Act 2003, which came into power in 2007. The case in question was that of armed robbery with the case commencing on Tuesday 12th January 2010.

Appeals in criminal cases

The defendant can appeal against conviction to the Court of Appeal (Criminal Division). The appeal must be lodged verbally at the court or within 14 days of the sentence in writing. A notice of appeal must be lodged with the Court of Appeal within 28 days. The Criminal Appeal Act 1995 states that the Court of Appeal:

a) shall allow an appeal against conviction if they think that the conviction is unsafe; and
b) shall dismiss such an appeal in any other case.

The Court of Appeal can allow an appeal and quash the conviction, vary the sentence, or overturn the appeal. A re-trial can also be ordered with a new jury. The prosecution also has limited rights of appeal. In the case of jury tampering an appeal against a not guilty finding is allowed. In addition, under s36 of the Criminal Justice Act 1972 the Attorney General can refer a point of law to the Court of Appeal. The decision does not affect the acquittal but can influence future law. Under s36 of the Criminal Justice Act 1988 the Attorney general can apply for leave to refer what is considered to be an unduly lenient sentence to the Court of Appeal for re-sentencing.

Appeals to the Supreme Court
Both prosecution and defence may appeal from the Court of Appeal to the Supreme Court. However, it is necessary to get the case certified as involving a point of law of general public importance, either from the Court of appeal or the Supreme Court.

Sentencing
Judges and magistrates have a fairly wide discretion when it comes to passing sentence on a guilty party, although they are subject to certain restrictions. Magistrates can only impose a maximum of six months imprisonment for one offence and twelve months for two. The Criminal Justice Act 2003 provides powers to increase the sentence for one offence to 12 months and two or more offences 15 months. The Legal Aid, Sentencing and Punishment of Offenders Act 2012 has also introduced new sentencing guidelines as well as other changes to the legal system, notably legal aid and youth sentencing. Judges in the

Crown Court can impose up to life imprisonment for some crimes and there is no maximum figure for fines.

There are certain other restrictions placed on the Magistrates and Crown Courts by Parliament. The maximum sentence to be handed out varies depending on the crime and Parliament determines the length of sentences.

Murder carries a mandatory life sentence, whereas the judge can work within the parameters of maximum of life for other crimes such as rape and manslaughter.

When judges or magistrates pass sentence, they will look at what they are trying to achieve when sentencing. Section 142 of the Criminal Justice Act 2003 sets out the purpose of sentencing for those aged 18 and over. This states that the court must have regard to:

- the punishment of offenders
- the reduction of crime
- the reform and rehabilitation of offenders
- the protection of the public
- the making of reparation by offenders to persons affected by their offences.

Courts have several different types of sentences available to them. There are four main categories: custodial sentences, community sentences, fines and discharges.

Custodial sentences
This is imprisonment and is the most serious sentence that a court can pass. Prison can range from a weekend to life. Custodial sentences include:

- mandatory and discretionary life sentences
- fixed term sentences
- short term sentences
- intermittent custody
- suspended sentences

Community sentences

Prior to the Criminal Justice Act 2003, the courts had individual community sentences that they could impose on an offender. The Act created one community order under which the courts can combine any requirements that they think are necessary. These requirements include all the previous existing community sentences that become available as 'requirements' or sentences required to rehabilitate the offender, and can be attached to the sentence.

The sentence is available for offenders of 16 or over. The full list of 'requirements' is set out in s 177 of the Criminal Justice Act 2003 which states:

177 (1) Where a person aged 16 or over is convicted of an offence, the court by or before which he is convicted may make an order imposing on him any one or more of the following requirements:

    a) an unpaid work requirement
    b) an activity requirement
    c) a programme requirement
    d) a prohibited activity requirement
    e) a curfew requirement
    f) an exclusion requirement

g) a residence requirement
h) a mental health treatment requirement
i) a drug rehabilitation requirement
j) an alcohol treatment requirement
k) a supervision requirement
l) in the case where an offender is under 25, an attendance centre requirement.

Fines
Legal Aid, Sentencing and Punishment of Offenders Act 2012

Magistrates can now issue much higher penalties on offenders who have committed the most serious 'Level Five' offences. The move will give magistrates more flexibility when deciding on punishments – they will still be able to hand down prison sentences of up to 6 months and be able to refer more serious cases to a Crown Court if they think a longer jail term is necessary.

In 2012 the government changed the law to give magistrates more powers to fine offenders. The March 2015 change's removes the upper limit on all current fines and maximum fines of £5,000 and above in the magistrates courts. Some examples of offences that will be included are:

- manufacture, import and sale of realistic imitation firearms - maximum penalty of 6 months in prison or a Level Five fine
- selling, supplying, offering to supply and hiring products to persons under 18, such as adult fireworks, crossbows/knives/axes/blades - maximum penalty of 6 month in prison or a Level Five fine

- sale of alcohol to children - maximum penalty of 6 months in prison or a Level Five fine
- unauthorised sale of (football) tickets - maximum penalty of 6 months in prison or a Level Five fine
- harassment (without violence) - maximum penalty of 6 months in prison or a Level Five fine)
- making false statement or representation to obtain social security benefit - maximum penalty of 3 months in prison or a Level Five fine
- failure to comply with an improvement notice to ensure properties are safe and habitable – maximum penalty of a Level Five fine

Sentencing is a matter for the independent judiciary, based on the full facts of the case. When handing down any fines magistrates will still take into account the financial means of the offender according to the sentencing guidelines.

Discharges

A discharge can be conditional or absolute. Conditional discharge means that the discharge is on condition that no further offence is committed in a set period up to three years. An absolute discharge means that no penalty has been imposed.

Other powers available to the courts

Courts can order compensation to a victim of crime. In the Magistrates court the maximum compensation is £5,000. If the defendant still has the property that he took from the victim then the court can order that it be returned. This is called a restitution order. A court can order that a person be deprived of property that he has used to commit the offence. There is special power to order forfeiture in drug related cases. The Proceeds of Crime Act 2002 also gives the courts powers to take from criminals all profits from crime for up to six years before conviction.

The Serious Crime Act 2015

The Serious Crime Act received Royal Assent on 3 March 2015. It amends and supplements the Proceeds of Crime Act 2002. The act gives effect to a number of proposals set out in the Serious and Organised Crime Strategy. It builds on the current criminal and civil law to ensure that the National Crime Agency, the police and other law enforcement agencies can continue effectively and relentlessly to pursue, disrupt and bring to justice serious and organised criminals. The act also introduces measures to enhance the protection of vulnerable children and others, including by strengthening the law to tackle female genital mutilation (FGM) and domestic abuse. The act also includes provisions to tighten prison security and to guard against the threat of terrorism.

The Act:
- improves the ability to recover criminal assets by amending the Proceeds of Crime Act 2002
- amends the Computer Misuse Act 1990 to ensure sentences for attacks on computer systems fully reflect the damage they cause
- creates a new offence targeting people who knowingly participate in an organised crime group
- extends the scope of serious crime prevention orders and gang injunctions creates new powers to seize, detain and

- destroy chemical substances suspected of being used as cutting agents for illegal drugs
- clarifies the offence of child cruelty in section 1 of the Children and Young Persons Act 1933, making it explicit that the offence covers cruelty which causes psychological suffering or injury as well as physical harm
- replaces anachronisticreferences to child prostitution and child pornography in the Sexual Offences Act 2003restricts the offence of loitering or soliciting for the purposes of prostitution to adults and introduces a new offence of sexual communication with a child
- creates a new offence making it illegal to possess paedophile manuals
- criminalises patterns of repeated or continuous coercive or controlling behaviour against an intimate partner or family member
- strengthens prison security by creating new offences of unauthorised possession of a knife or other offensive weapon in prison and throwing articles into a prison
- gives courts the power to make mobile network operators disconnect mobile communication devices being used in prison without authorisation
- allows people suspected of committing an offence overseas under sections 5 (preparation of terrorism acts) or 6 (training for terrorism) of the Terrorism Act 2006 to be prosecuted in the UK

Offenders who are mentally ill

The law recognises, as far as it possibly can, that mentally ill offenders should receive treatment as opposed to punishment.

Courts have a wide range of powers available to them when dealing with such offenders. The main extra powers available to courts are to give the offender a community sentence with a requirement that he or she attends for treatment, make a hospital order or to make a restriction order under the Mental Health Act 1983 section 41.

Under the same section, offenders with severe mental health problems can be sent to high security hospitals such as Broadmoor. Such an order can only be made by the Crown Court.

Anti-social behaviour orders

A person can get a civil injunction, Community Protection Notice (CPN) or Criminal Behaviour Order (CBO) as punishment for antisocial behaviour.

Civil injunctions, CPNs and CBOs replaced Antisocial Behaviour Orders (ASBOs) in England, Wales and Northern Ireland. ASBOs are still used in Scotland. Antisocial behaviour includes:

- drunken or threatening behaviour
- vandalism and graffiti
- playing loud music at night

A court may give a civil injunction or a CPN if it gets reports of persistent antisocial behaviour from the police, a council or a landlord. A person can only get a CBO if they have been convicted of a crime. A person can get a civil injunction or CBO if they are 10 or over and a CPN if 16 or over. A person must follow certain rules or they could get a more severe punishment such as:

- stay away from a particular place, like a local town centre
- stop spending time with certain people
- work on improving behaviour, for example by going to a support group
- fix damage caused to someone's property

There's no maximum amount of time a CPN can last. How long civil injunctions and CBOs can last depends on age.
- a CBO lasts between 12 months and 3 years
- There's no maximum amount of time if a person is 18 or over.
- If they have a CBO it'll be reviewed every year and either stopped or extended.

The punishment for not following a civil injunction is:
- a 3 month detention order if under 18
- up to 2 years' imprisonment or unlimited fine if 18 or over
- The punishment for not following a CPN is a fine between £100 and £2,500.

The punishment for not following a CBO is:
- up to 2 years in a detention centre if under 18
- up to 5 years in prison or an unlimited fine (or both) if 18 or over

New sentencing guidelines for magistrates' courts published

The Sentencing Council has published revised guidelines for offences in the Magistrates' Court Sentencing Guidelines. The guidelines apply to all offenders aged 18 and older who are sentenced on or after 24 April 2017, regardless of the date of the offence. For details of these guidelines go to www.sentencingcouncil.org.uk.

****

Index

Abortion, 6, 71
Actual Bodily Harm, 7, 87
Actus reus, 6, 48, 82
Age and lack of capacity, 9
Aggravated burglary, 8, 110
Aggravated criminal damage, 8, 112, 115, 151
Animal Welfare, 9, 18, 138, 142
Anti-social behaviour orders, 13, 203
Anti-Terrorism, Crime and Security Act 2001, 164
Arrest for breach of the peace, 169
Arrestable offences, 11, 167
Arson, 8, 40, 112, 115
Assault, 6, 40, 81

Bail, 180
Bail Act 1976, 41, 180, 186
Battery, 6, 84, 85
Binding precedent, 3, 25
Burglary, 7, 45, 107

Caldwell recklessness, 5, 55
Causation, 5, 48
Chain of causation, 6, 64
Child Sexual Offences, 137
Citizens Advice Bureau, 172
Commission for Equality and Human Rights, 172
Common law, 3, 21, 22, 39
Community sentences, 12, 198
Community Support Officers, 172
Complaints against the police, 172

Computer Misuse Act 1990, 116
Conspiracy to commit a crime, 10, 157
Constructive manslaughter, 6, 73
Corporate manslaughter, 6, 78
Corporate Manslaughter and Corporate Homicide Act, 78
County Court, 29
Court of Appeal, 24, 28, 29, 30, 48, 49, 51, 65, 66, 68, 70, 74, 75, 76, 78, 88, 104, 105, 107, 109, 113, 145, 146, 152, 154, 155, 157, 195, 196
COVID 19, 18
Crime and Disorder Act 1988, 191
Crime and Disorder Act 1998, 39, 148
Crime of basic intent, 5, 52
Crimes of specific intent, 5, 52
Criminal Appeal Act 1995, 195
Criminal Attempts Act 1981, 156, 157
Criminal damage, 8, 45, 111, 113
Criminal Damage Act 1971, 56, 111, 112, 113, 116, 152, 153
Criminal Justice Act 1988, 81, 196
Criminal Justice Act 2003, 162
Criminal Justice and Immigration Act 2008, 10, 153
Criminal Justice and Public Order Act 1994, 162, 164, 168, 171
Criminal Law Act 1967, 88, 143
Criminal negligence, 5, 57
Criminal Procedures (Insanity and Unfitness to Plead) Act 1991, 149
Crown Prosecution Service, 12, 178, 187
Cunningham recklessness, 5, 55
Custodial sentences, 12, 197
Customs, 3, 20
Cybercrime, 8, 9, 121, 128
Cyber-dependent crimes, 121
Cyber-enabled crimes, 121

Damage to computer programmes, 8, 116
Defining a crime, 4, 38
Diminished responsibility, 6, 66
Discharges, 13, 200
Duress, 10, 154

Elements of a crime, 4, 45
Equity, 3, 22
Establishing criminal liability, 4, 46
European Court of Justice, 27, 28

Factual causation, 5, 49
Fines, 12, 189, 199
Fingerprints, 171
Forgery and Counterfeiting Act 1981, 131
Fraud Act 2006, 103, 117, 119, 131, 132, 134

General customs, 3, 20

Hacking, 8, 122
High Court, 3, 28, 192
Homicide, 5, 62, 66, 67, 71, 78

Inchoate offences, 156
Indictable offences, 4, 40, 180
Indirect battery, 7, 85
Infanticide Act 1938, 71
Insanity, 9, 10, 149
Intellectual Property Crime, 9, 132
Intention, 5, 52, 158
Intoxication, 10, 151
Involuntary intoxication, 10, 151

Involuntary manslaughter, 6, 62, 72

Judicial precedents, 3, 23

Legal causation, 5, 49
Local customs, 3, 21
Loss of self-control, 6, 68

Magistrates, 180
Magistrates Court, 12, 29, 40, 45, 87, 112, 179, 180, 187, 188, 190, 191, 192
Malice aforethought, 6, 64
Malicious wounding, 7, 88
Malware, 123, 124
Manslaughter, 6, 40, 62, 77, 78
Marital coercion, 10, 155
Mens Rea, 5, 51
Mental Health Act 1983, 203
Mistakes about the law, 10, 152
Misuse of Drugs Act 1971, 164
Murder, 5, 39, 40, 52, 62, 63, 151, 197

Necessity, 10, 154
Negligence, 5, 57
Non-Insane Automatism, 10, 150

Obiter Dicta, 3, 24
Obscene Publications, 137
Offences against the Person Act 1861, 81
Offences Against the Person Act 1861, 71, 159
Online Safety Bill, 121, 134, 136
Original precedent, 3, 24

Parliament, 164, 167
Persuasive precedent, 3, 25
Police and Criminal Evidence Act (PACE) 1984, 162
Police powers, 11, 162
Powers of arrest, 11, 167
Powers to detain suspect, 11, 169
Powers to stop and search, 11, 163
Prosecution of Offences Act 1985, 187
Provocation, 6, 67

Rape, 40
Ratio Decidendi, 3, 23
Recklessness, 5, 54
Right to silence, 171
Rights of detained people, 170
Roadside checks, 11, 165
Robbery, 7, 40, 106

Search warrant, 166
Self-defence, 10, 152
Sentencing, 12, 196
Serious Crime and Police Act 2005, 161
Serious Organised Crime Agency (SOCA, 161
Sources of criminal law, 39
Strict liability, 5, 57
Suicide, 70
Summary Trials, 12, 189
Supreme Court, 3, 12, 28, 29, 192, 196

The Criminal Justice and Public Order Act 1994, 185
The Criminal Procedure (Amendment) Rules 2023, 41, 42, 181, 182
The Dangerous Dogs Act 1991, 9, 140

The doctrine of precedents, 3, 23
The Independent Police Complaints Commission, 172
The Mutilations Regulations 2007, 142
The Police Crime, Sentencing and Courts Act 2022, 175
The Public Order Act 2023, 176
The Welfare of Farmed Animals (England) Regulations 2007, 142
Theft, 7, 45, 46, 103, 105, 106, 107, 110, 112, 151, 152
Theft Act 1979, 103
Things in action, 7, 106
Transferred malice, 5, 57
Trespasser, 8, 110
Triable either-way offences, 4, 45, 179

Unlawful entry, 167
Unlawful entry and search, 11
Upskirting, 100

Voluntary manslaughter, 6, 62, 66
Voluntary searches, 11, 164

Withdrawal Act (WA) 2020, 27
Worms, 123

Youth courts, 12, 191

****